Jennifer Aldridge's ARCHERS' COOKBOOK

SEY

Jennifer Aldridge's

ARCHERS' COOKBOOK

dc
David & Charles

For Ben, Dan and Mimi with love

Uncle Walter's wisdom:
'Walk ten miles a day or
Maybe walk a score
And you'll never have a doctor
Knockin' at yer door.'

A DAVID & CHARLES BOOK

Illustrations by Sally Maltby

First published 1994

A catalogue record for this book is available from the British Library.

ISBN 0 7153 0141 1

Typeset by Greenshires Icon, Exeter
and printed in Great Britain by Butler & Tanner Ltd
for David & Charles,
Brunel House Newton Abbot Devon

CONTENTS

INTRODUCTION

Where is Ambridge? There's no secret about it! Tucked into a fold in the undulating South Borsetshire countryside, it nestles in the Vale of the Am, just six miles out of Borchester. It's more than just a village with a pub and a church and a pond on the green: it's a special place, touched by a certain sort of magic.

I have lived here for most of my life, married to Brian and surrounded by family, mainly farming folk, and friends. Writing has always been important to me. As well as my published short stories and regular contributions to the Borchester Echo, *I co-authored* Ambridge – an English Village through the Ages *with John Tregorran, a local historian. My other great joy, as Brian will testify, is entertaining at Home Farm. Elegant dinner parties on rather a lavish scale is, I suppose, how you might describe them.*

It was at one such occasion several years ago that the idea for this book was born – by accident really. It was all because Mandy Beeseborough was frightfully impressed by my fluffy 'Floating Islands'. Of course, Brian let the cat out of the bag, revealing that they were one of Caroline's clever concoctions. But might it not be a good idea if I were to compile a cookbook of all the recipes begged or borrowed from my gourmet friends? 'Keep you out of mischief darling!' he said, winking at Mandy. Keep me away from Underwood's Couture Range is what he really meant.

So what started with a chance comment that evening began to take shape in my mind as a fascinating project: to paint a wholesome epicurean portrait of Ambridge life.

Uncle Walter's wisdom:
'Now wine, rum and whisky are good if they're free
But there's value for money in beer and in tea.'

It has been a delight to discover such a wonderfully varied selection of cooking styles among my many friends in the village. All were only too happy to open their doors and welcome me into their kitchens to share their culinary secrets. Some of the recipes, as one would expect, are traditional, classic dishes, but many are surprisingly new and exciting, and reflect the character of the cooks who have contributed ideas.

Some glory in the simplicity of country fare using the hedgerow's free bounty. Others are more sophisticated, with unusual and exotic ingredients available only in Underwood's Fine Food Department. All of them are delicious.

I have tried to evoke the countryside using natural flavours, capture the feel of the village with its mouthwatering aromas, reflect the changing seasons, the country festivals and seasonal feasts. On a crisp and frosty winter's day I want you to feel you can warm your toes by the crackling logs in Brookfield's hearth and see the flames reflected in Jill's polished brass as you bite into those buttery toasted hot cross buns. I would like you to smell the sweet scented bunches of rosemary and

Uncle Walter's wisdom:
'No matter how humble, how rough or how rude
A man should be willing to show gratitude.'

thyme strung from low beams in Shula's rush-seated sitting room, or to imagine lying by the Lower Loxley lake on a summer's day, wicker hamper opened wide offering tempting picnic treats.

Or perhaps you would prefer to sample Jean-Paul's exquisitely presented cuisine. His smart menu, in French of course, is redolent of Grey Gables' fleur-de-lys flock papered dining room, with its stiff napkins perched on plates like bishops' mitres, and cutlery and glass gleaming and sparkling.

Uncle Walter's wisdom:
'Be out in the fields when the sun shines bright
And keep all yer sleep for the dark hours of night.'

Uncle Walter's wisdom:
'When the elm leaf's like a mouse's ear
Then sew yer barley, never fear.'

Uncle Walter's wisdom:
'To cure rheumatism carry a large turnip with you under yer coat.'

You may like to work off your rich repast with a virtuous climb, pink-cheeked and puffing, to the summit of Lakey Hill. There should be plenty of time for a visit to the Bridge Farm shop – stacked with crunchy, slightly muddy vegetables. You'll need your wellies to pick your way across the Grundys' scruffy yard, but Clarrie will welcome you at the kitchen door, sleeves rolled up and arms akimbo, to home baked bread and warming soup.

But whatever you choose to do first, I insist that when the time comes for you to put on your striped apron, pick up your large wooden spoon and begin to stir the rich dark fruity mixture of Jill Archer's spicy Christmas pudding, you don't forget to make a wish. I hope you'll wish that you really are *in Ambridge.*

ACKNOWLEDGEMENTS

My thanks go to Owen Bentley, Vanessa Whitburn and The Archers office team for their help and co-operation, and to my editor Sue Hall for her patience and reassurance.

I am also exceedingly grateful to my husband Peter, my family and the many friends, including Penny and Shelagh of 'Fodders', who have contributed ideas and sampled recipes.

My special thanks go to all Ambridge's inhabitants, without whose existence this book would not have been possible.

HOME FARM

'THERE'S NO SIGNPOST, I KNOW, but it's terribly easy to find. Look out for our field of deer on the Little Croxley road, then turn left by that enormous oak and we're there, at the end of a long, straight drive.'

Wisteria and clematis-clad, quintessentially Country Life, *so graciously Georgian, with perfect rows of well-proportioned windows set in softly weathered Borsetshire brick. Just try not to notice those big, ugly barns and looming silo – it is a farmstead after all.*

'Park in the cobbled yard if you can.' By the side of Brian's busy office with its chattering fax machine and puzzle-solving computers. That'll keep the concrete hub of the working farm clear, where tractors and balers, trailers and lorries are constantly manoeuvring.

'And let yourself in by the back door.' You'll have to fight your way through a rainforest of green thornproofs and tangle-welly'd undergrowth to get to the heart of my home – that warm kitchen, where a rustic dresser leans against the wall, plates propped and cups dangling, its porcelain-knobbed drawers jammed with worthless treasures.

There's the pompously bright red Aga, harbouring soothing childhood memories of night-time treats – mugs of milky chocolate and rounds of butter-dripping toast. The Sunday smells of crackling-coated roasts and bubbling freshly minted new potatoes. And those decadently late, lingering breakfasts – coffee pots perking, newspapers crumby from rich croissants spread with syrupy spoonfuls of lumpy ginger conserve and stone-free greengage jam.

'Follow me through to the drawing room.' Grey and windy weekend afternoons are spent here in feather-cushioned comfort by a

glowing fruit-wood fire, lost in the mysteries of Mah-jong, or engrossed in a paperback novel. The only permitted interruption arrives in the form of a chinking tray laden with hunks of spicy farmhouse fruit cake and a scalding pot of delicately scented tea.

Frosty crisp days find the girls smart in their hacking jackets on brisk country rides, their soft-muzzled ponies trotting down tree-lined bridleways, through Leaders Wood and Lyttleton Cover, and along by the side of our trout-rich lake.

Alice and I go winter walking, making the most of nature's bounty, picking armfuls of berried branches and trailing evergreens, returning home before the fast-fading twilight.

In late summer, simple suppers on the terrace by the limpid pool, crisp herby salads with sharp lemon dressings and fresh tasting, tangy summer fruits.

The mournful, mellow days of autumn, when pheasant shooting starts, find me cheerfully chopping and peeling, stirring bubbling cauldrons of pickles and chunky vinegary chutneys.

It was into this seemingly idyllic life that I married some twenty years ago, a troubled and struggling single parent, with a failed marriage, two small children, no money, not knowing what to do next or which way to go. It still seems a miracle that I met Brian, a privileged and wealthy bachelor, and my new husband-to-be. He had recently sold his family's home and land, extremely lucratively too, and bought outright, 'with cash' as they say, Home Farm and more than half the acreage of the best farming land in Ambridge.

Now, my children growing up and leaving home, I find myself with idle hands, and needing a worthwhile project to fill my long and otherwise lazy days. With this in mind I started collecting handed-down recipes from families in the village, with the idea of compiling a book of Ambridge's culinary and epicurean delights.

☆ HOME FARM POOLSIDE LUNCH PARTY ☆

With Kate whining on about 'Interrailing' and Debbie and Brian indulging in their memories of France, I decided on a Mediterranean, by-the-pool, hoping-the-sun-shines, lunch party.

It was huge fun preparing the food – the smell of garlic and olive oil made me feel as though I were halfway up a mountain in Andalucia. I cooked the chicken in the Aga, in case of a downpour, and even swept out my 3J's studio. Initially we had to force the girls to invite their chums, but I think they enjoyed it too.

MEDITERRANEAN OLIVE PÂTÉ

SERVES 6

A sophisticated starter, this is something a bit different from the rather tedious taramasalata.

7oz (200g) pitted black olives
2 anchovy fillets
2oz (50g) capers, rinsed
1 clove garlic
1tbsp lemon juice
pinch of thyme
1tbsp brandy or rum
2tbsp olive oil
pinch of dry mustard
black pepper

Strain the black olives, if using tinned ones. Peel and chop the garlic, drain the anchovy fillets. Put the olives, garlic, anchovies, capers, brandy, lemon juice and thyme into a liquidiser and blend to a rough paste. Stir in the olive oil and add the black pepper and mustard powder. Store in a screw-top jar for 2 to 3 days.

Serve on strips of warm, crisp white bread – ciabatta if you can get it.

A tip for Betty Tucker – Hand wash forks, knives and fish servers, adding dried mustard powder or vinegar to the water to remove the smell of fish!

SUNNY CARROT AND ORANGE SALAD

SERVES 6–8 AS A SIDE SALAD

Brightly coloured and delicately flavoured, and the mustard seeds make this salad special.

1tbsp olive oil
2tsp black mustard seeds
4 Jaffa oranges
2lb (1kg) young carrots
2tsp chopped fresh parsley
2oz (50g) raisins

Heat the olive oil and fry the black mustard seeds until they pop, then allow to cool. Squeeze the juice from one orange and add to the mustard seeds. Peel the other three oranges and segment them into pith-free pieces. Scrub and coarsely grate the carrots.

Combine all the ingredients and toss in the mustard seeds, olive oil and orange juice.

SPICY RICE

SERVES 6–8

Nutty, glossy and golden – almost a meal in itself. With some prawns scattered over it, it could be just that.

2tbsp cooking oil
1oz (25g) butter or margarine
2 medium onions, finely chopped
2 cloves garlic, crushed
1tsp ground cumin
1tsp ground coriander
1tsp ground cinnamon
1tsp turmeric
12oz (350g) long-grain, easy-cook rice
12fl oz (350ml) vegetable stock
salt and white pepper
6oz (175g) almond flakes, toasted

Melt the oil and butter in a large, heavy-bottomed pan and fry the onion until soft and golden. Add the garlic and all the spices and continue frying for another minute or two. Stir in the rinsed rice and add the vegetable stock.

Season with salt (not too much if the stock is already salty) and pepper, cover the pan with a well-fitting lid and simmer gently for 10–12 minutes, until all the liquid has been absorbed and the rice is cooked.

Stir in the freshly toasted almonds, transfer to a serving dish and serve hot or cold.

CRISPY LEMON AND LIME CHICKEN

SERVES 6

Plenty of paper napkins are needed here as everyone ends up eating this with their fingers.

6 chicken portions
2 garlic cloves, crushed
1tbsp ground ginger
3-4tbsp extra virgin olive oil
4 limes, the juice and 1tsp zest
2 lemons, the juice and 1tsp zest
1tbsp clear honey
1tbsp honey mustard
1tbsp chopped coriander leaves

Place the chicken pieces in a large bowl, and add the garlic, ginger, olive oil and the juice of the lemons and limes. Combine and leave to marinate for 24 hours.

Drain the chicken pieces (reserving the marinade) and place on a baking tray. Bake for 25–35 minutes at 400°F/200°C/Gas 6 or until the chicken is tender and browned.

Place the reserved marinade in a saucepan with the honey, honey mustard and zest of the lemons and limes and boil until it becomes thick and syrupy.

To serve, place the chicken portions in a serving dish, pour over the marinade, sprinkle with chopped coriander and garnish with lemon wedges.

Aubergine, Tomato and Green Lentil Salad

SERVES 6–8

A salad with a difference – and with green lentils being the 'designer' ingredient at the moment it has *to be a success!*

4oz (100g) Puy (green) lentils, soaked overnight
4 medium aubergines, about 6oz (175g) each
4 large tomatoes, skinned and chopped
1 green pepper, deseeded and chopped
1 small onion, chopped

FOR THE DRESSING
6tbsp olive oil
juice of 2 lemons
3 garlic cloves, crushed
3tbsp fresh coriander leaves, chopped
2tsp cumin
½tsp cayenne pepper
1tsp salt

Drain the soaked lentils, cover with fresh water and cook for 30 minutes or until soft. Drain and cool.

Prick the skins of the aubergines and bake at 400°F/200°C/Gas 6 until they are soft and the skins are crinkly. Allow them to cool, then peel. Chop the flesh coarsely into a bowl and add the skinned and chopped tomatoes, lentils, chopped pepper and onion.

To make the dressing, mix the spices and seasoning together with the oil and lemon juice. Add to the aubergines, stirring in some of the coriander, leaving a little to garnish.

Tiramisù

SERVES 8

Absolutely the *thing to choose at any Wandsworth Wine Bar or Battersea Bistro – it's very rich. I think they eat it in Rome too!*

10fl oz (275ml/ ½pt) strong black coffee
2tbsp coffee liqueur or brandy
24 crisp boudoir sponge finger biscuits
3 medium size eggs, separated
3tbsp caster sugar
2 × 9oz (250g) cartons mascarpone cheese
a little cocoa powder

Mix the coffee and liqueur together. Immerse the sponge fingers in the mixture one at a time, then line the bottom of a glass trifle bowl with half of them.

Whisk or beat the egg yolks with the sugar until pale and thick. Add the mascarpone gradually until the mixture is evenly blended. Whisk the egg whites until they stand in stiff peaks then fold into the mascarpone mixture.

Spread half the mixture over the sponge fingers in the trifle bowl, then add another layer of coffee-soaked sponge fingers and spread the remaining mascarpone on top.

Decorate liberally with sifted cocoa powder and chill overnight, or for at least 6 hours. Serve chilled.

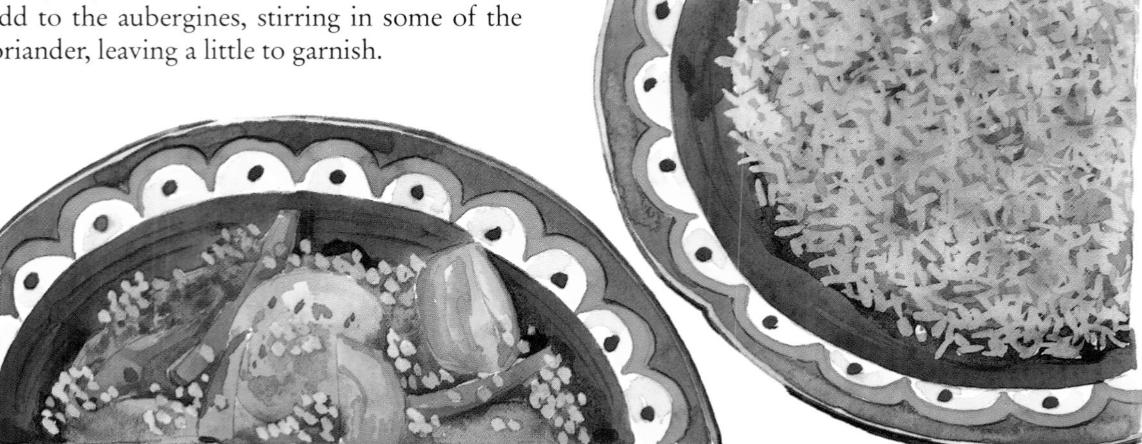

☆ HOME FARM DINNER PARTY ☆

A surprisingly easy dinner party menu with each dish prepared well beforehand – leaving heaps of time to chase Alice up to bed, dig Brian out of the lambing sheds, check that the bone handles are still on the fish knives (Betty Tucker would keep putting them in the dishwasher!) and sink down into a favourite chair with a well-earned sherry for a quick glance at Country Life.

TROUT MOUSSE WITH LEMON AND WHISKY

SERVES 8–10 AS A STARTER

This delicately flavoured mousse can be made with fresh salmon if you prefer. I think I do, but Brian would be frightfully miffed if I didn't use his wretched rainbow trout.

10fl oz (275ml/ ½pt) fish stock
1 sachet (½oz/12g) powdered gelatine
1lb (450g) cooked trout, boned and flaked
10fl oz (275ml/ ½pt) mayonnaise
2tbsp whisky (optional) or lemon juice
grated rind of 2 lemons
10fl oz (275ml/½pt) whipping cream
salt and white or lemon pepper

Bring the fish stock to the boil, scatter on the gelatine and stir until dissolved. Leave to cool but not set.

In a food processor or blender make a soft, smooth purée of the flaked trout with the fish jelly. Add the mayonnaise, whisky, lemon rind and seasoning and combine thoroughly.

Whip the cream until it forms soft peaks and fold carefully into the fish mixture. Pour into individual ramekin dishes or one large serving dish and chill for 4–5 hours. Garnish with watercress and lemon wedges and serve with brown toast.

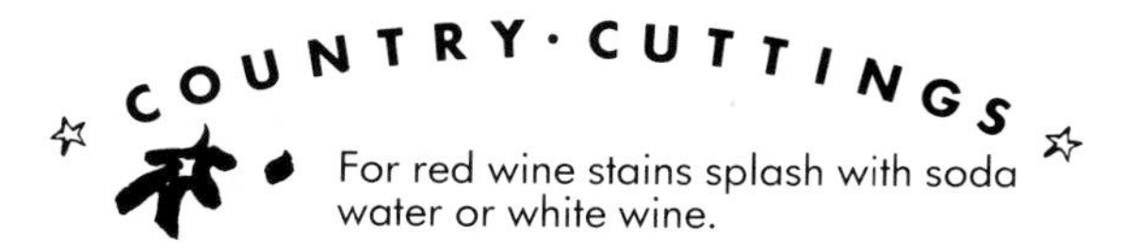

For red wine stains splash with soda water or white wine.

VENISON AND PHEASANT CASSEROLE

SERVES 4–6

This rich casserole is a delectable combination of our home produce and a wonderful way to entice new customers. It can serve up to 6 people, depending on the size of the pheasants – and people's appetites!

2lb (1kg) haunch of venison, sliced and cut into bite-size cubes
3 pheasant breasts, sliced into slivers
2 large onions, chopped
1 plump garlic clove, crushed
sprig of sage, chopped
1tsp honey mustard
1 bottle red wine
olive oil for frying

FOR THE MARINADE
3tbsp olive oil
4 garlic cloves, crushed
2tbsp juniper berries, crushed
rind and juice of 2 oranges
salt and pepper

Mix together all the ingredients for the marinade, adding half the bottle of red wine, place in two covered bowls and marinate the venison and pheasant separately overnight. Remove the venison and pheasant from the marinade, pat dry on absorbent kitchen roll and keep separate. Strain and reserve the marinade.

In a large frying pan heat 1tbsp of olive oil and quickly fry the venison until browned on all sides. Remove to an ovenproof casserole.

Fry the pheasant breast slices in the pan over a fairly high heat until just browned on both sides, then remove to a separate dish. Add a little more oil to the pan and fry the onions and garlic for about a minute. Transfer to the casserole containing the venison. Add the sage, the remainder of the bottle of wine and the reserved marinade to the casserole. Stir in the honey mustard and season.

Place in a moderate oven at 325°F/160°C/Gas 3 and cook for 1 hour, then add the pheasant breast. Continue cooking for another hour, or until the meat is tender.

Pour the casserole juices into a saucepan, skim off the fat and boil briskly to thicken the sauce. Pour over the meat, cover and keep warm until ready to serve with roast parsnips, parboiled and baked in cooking oil and butter for 45 minutes at 375°F/190°C/Gas 5, until brown all over.

BAKED GARLIC POTATOES

This is a favourite way of cooking baked potatoes.

Choose potatoes weighing about 3oz (75g) each. Scrub the skins thoroughly and rub liberally with olive oil and sea salt. Place in a large ovenproof casserole, preferably earthenware, and scatter at least a dozen unpeeled garlic cloves into the casserole. Drizzle in a little extra oil, replace the lid and bake for about 1¼ hours at 350°F/180°C/Gas 4. The cooked garlic cloves, with their creamy centres, can be served with the potatoes.

BEETROOT PURÉE

SERVES 3–4

Beetroot is a vegetable which is undeservedly ignored – perhaps it's the colour that proves off-putting. Here it's subtly earthy and unsubtly red.

1oz (25g) butter
1 large onion, finely chopped
1lb (450g) beetroot, cooked, peeled and chopped
1 plump garlic clove, crushed
2 medium cooking apples, peeled, cored and chopped
salt, pepper
½tsp powdered mace

Heat the butter and fry the onion over a low heat until transparent. Add the chopped beetroot, garlic, and apple and simmer over a low heat until amalgamated into a thick purée. Season with salt, freshly ground pepper and mace.

BOMBE SURPRISE WITH APRICOT SAUCE AND ALMOND PRALINE

SERVES 4–6

Brian says this tastes much better than it looks – hence the name. If you don't have the time or the patience to make the meringues, bought ones will work equally well. Break them into pieces and pop them briefly under a hot grill to brown .

3 medium egg whites
6oz (175g) caster sugar
15fl oz (425ml/¾pt) double cream
2oz (50g) dried no-soak apricots
3tbsp almond liqueur (amaretto)
1tbsp (heaped) sifted icing sugar

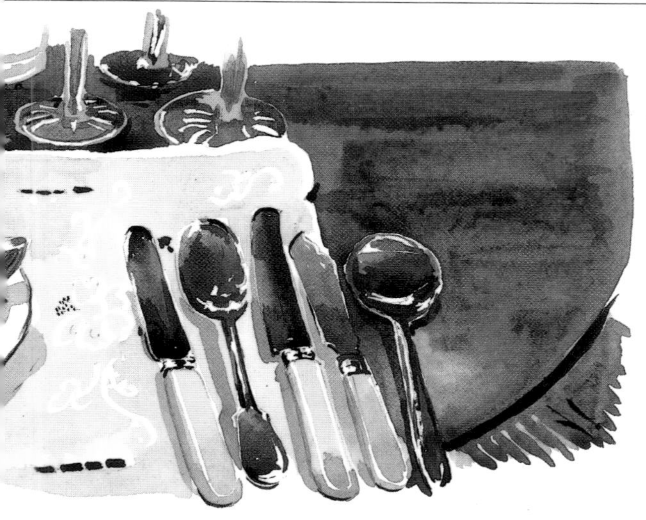

To make the meringues, whisk the egg whites until stiff, gradually whisk in half of the caster sugar, folding in the remainder with a spatula or a metal spoon. Spoon the meringue into heaps on to an oiled baking sheet. Bake in a very slow oven at 200°F/100°C for about 2 hours. When cool remove from the baking sheet and break into small pieces.

Whip the cream until fairly stiff, forming light peaks.

Chop the apricots finely. Fold the apricots, liqueur, icing sugar and meringue into the cream.

Lightly oil a bombe mould, or line with cling film. (Alternatively, you can use a 2¼pt pudding basin.) Spoon in the creamy mixture, cover with foil and freeze for at least 5 hours.

To serve, dip the mould/basin briefly into a sink of hot water and turn out on to a plate. Leave for 8–10 minutes before serving.

To make the apricot sauce, pour hot water over 8oz (225g) apricots and soak for 1 hour. Drain and place in a pan with 1oz (25g) caster sugar, the juice of 1 lemon and 10fl oz (275ml/½pt) water. Boil, and simmer until soft, then sieve or blend in a food processor. Pour back into the rinsed pan, add the amaretto if desired, and heat gently. The sauce can also be served cold.

To make the almond praline, heat 4oz (100g) caster sugar and 2tbsp water in a thick-bottomed saucepan, and boil gently without stirring until it becomes a thick, golden-brown syrup. Remove from the heat and stir in the almonds. Grease a board with butter and pour on the mixture; cool, then crush with a rolling pin. Sprinkle on the bombe before serving. The praline should be stored in an airtight tin.

LANGUES DE-CHAT

MAKES ABOUT 16 BISCUITS

Vivacious Marie-Claire gave us the recipe for these typical French biscuits – the shape of a cat's tongue – when she stayed at Home Farm during the first town-twinning visit. Alice, clad in a large apron, insists on helping. She adores dipping the biscuits into the chocolate – well, she actually prefers licking her fingers afterwards.

2½oz (65g) unsalted butter
2½oz (65g) caster sugar
1tsp vanilla essence
2 large unbeaten egg whites
2½oz (65g) plain flour, sifted
a pinch of salt
3oz (75g) plain chocolate

Soften the butter, and cream together with the sugar and vanilla essence. Beat in the egg whites one at a time. Stir in the sifted flour and salt. Pipe the mixture through a ½in piping nozzle on to greased baking sheets. Make the biscuits about 2–3in long and space well apart.

Bake in a preheated oven at 400°F/200°C/Gas 6 for about 6–7 minutes or until the biscuits are golden-brown around the edges. Cool on a wire rack.

Melt the chocolate in a basin over a pan of hot water. When the biscuits are cool, dip the ends into the melted chocolate. Place on greaseproof paper to set.

LAMB, LEEK AND PRUNE PIES

MAKES 8 SMALL PIES

In Victorian times the hunting lodges prepared traditional feasts for the gentry to enjoy in style and reasonable comfort. How then could I provide only the odd flask of coffee for the guns and beaters? These savoury meat pies are welcome served with hot soup on Brian's pheasant shoots.

FOR THE HOT WATER CRUST PASTRY
1lb (450g) plain flour
1tsp salt
7oz (200g) lard
7fl oz (200ml) water (approximately)

FOR THE FILLING
1tbsp sunflower oil
1 medium onion, finely chopped
1lb (450g) lamb, best neck fillet, trimmed and cubed
2 plump garlic cloves, finely chopped
3oz (75g) prunes, stoned and chopped
1 sprig rosemary, chopped
1 leek, chopped
salt and pepper

To make the hot water crust pastry, sieve the flour and salt together in a bowl. Make a well in the centre. In a saucepan melt the lard in the water and bring to the boil, then pour into the well. Beat the mixture quickly to make a soft dough. Knead until a pliable dough is formed, adding a little extra flour if necessary. Leave covered for half an hour to allow the dough to become more elastic.

To make the pie filling, heat the oil in a large frying pan and fry the onion until translucent. Add the meat and garlic and fry until brown. Add the prunes and rosemary, cover and cook for 10 minutes. Finally, stir in the leek and seasoning and cook for a further 2–3 minutes. Spread the mixture on a plate and allow to cool.

Divide the pastry into 8 pieces and use two-thirds of each piece to line a 4in (10cm) individual quiche or Yorkshire pudding tin. Roll out the remaining one-thirds to form pastry lids. Spoon the cooled meat mixture into the tins, moisten the edges of the pastry and press down the pastry lids. Brush the lids with oil and pierce a hole in the centre. Bake in a preheated oven at 350°F/180°C/Gas 4 for 30–40 minutes until brown.

PARSNIP, POTATO AND NUTMEG SOUP

SERVES 6–8

This is a heartwarming soup that I put in vacuum flasks and take out to the shoot on chilly winter days. It is improved enormously by the addition of a glass or two of good Amontillado.

2lb (1kg) parsnips, diced
2 large potatoes, chopped
3 large onions, chopped
40fl oz (1.2L/2pt) vegetable stock
salt, pepper
freshly grated nutmeg

Simmer the vegetables in 30fl oz (900ml/1½pt) of the stock for about 35 minutes or until tender. Purée the soup in a blender or food processor. Add the remaining stock, salt, pepper and a generous sprinkling of nutmeg.

Serve with hot garlic bread or granary rolls.

PADDINGTON'S PUDDING

FEEDS ONE HUNGRY CHILD!

This was a great favourite of Adam's many years ago – and now of Alice's. Brian prefers a more sophisticated version, spreading the bread with peach conserve and using cinnamon sugar.

2 slices white bread
a little lemon marmalade
a little butter
a little caster sugar

Butter the bread and make a marmalade sandwich. Cut off the crusts and cut into four triangles. Melt a little butter in a frying pan and fry the sandwiches until golden on both sides. Dust with sugar and serve with a dollop of cream.

EARL GREY FRUIT CAKE

Lady Goodman kindly gave this recipe to me one evening when she and Sir Sidney were having dinner with us. It's moist and delicately flavoured with oil of Bergamot – just the cake to impress a visiting great-aunt at tea on the lawn.

2oz (50g) Earl Grey tea
10oz (275g) sultanas
10oz (275g) currants
4oz (100g) margarine
3oz (75g) butter
7oz (200g) soft dark brown sugar
3 medium size eggs
7oz (200g) self-raising flour
2oz (50g) ground almonds
4oz (100g) glacé cherries, halved
4oz (100g) mixed peel
4oz (100g) walnuts, halved

Infuse tea in 10fl oz (275ml/½pt) boiling water for 1 hour, then drain. Soak the sultanas and currants in the tea mixture for at least 9 hours.

Cream the margarine, butter and sugar. Add the eggs slowly and, with the last one, add a little flour. Fold in the rest of the flour, ground almonds, cherries, mixed peel, walnuts and the tea-soaked fruit. Grease and line an 8in cake tin and bake in a preheated oven at 300°F/150°C/Gas 2 for 3–3¼ hours. Test with a skewer, which should come away clean. Cool in the tin before turning out on to a wire rack.

HUNGRY HUNTER'S CAKE *for Debbie* or FAMISHED FARMER'S CAKE *for Brian*

Debbie used to say this was just the cake to be eaten after a healthy day's hunting – or a day at the 'off-the-road' riding course. Don't be discouraged if it sinks in the middle. I cut it in hefty chunks and offer it with hot coffee for a shooting lunch. It can also be spread with butter.

12oz (350g) margarine
9oz (250g) demerara sugar
4 medium size eggs
grated rind and juice of 1 orange
2tbsp clear honey
15oz (425g) self-raising flour
2oz (50g) cocoa powder
1tsp mixed spice
8oz (225g) mixed peel
12oz (350g) seedless raisins

Cream together the margarine and sugar until soft. Beat together the eggs, orange juice and honey, and gradually beat into the creamed mixture, with a little flour to prevent curdling. Fold in the rest of the sifted flour, cocoa, mixed spice and orange rind. Finally, stir in the mixed peel and raisins.

Place in a greased and lined 9in cake tin. Cook at 325°F/160°C/Gas 3 for about 2–2½ hours, testing with a skewer to check that the mixture is cooked through. Cool in the tin before turning out on to a wire rack.

BROOKFIELD FARM

PICTURE A CHILD'S COLOURING BOOK. There's a farm, and that farm is Brookfield, with pigs and cows and sheep. Hens are scratching in the yard, and the be-aproned farmer's wife is scattering corn gleaned from the golden September fields. The mellow brick walls of the farmhouse, under the moss-mottled roof, are dappled with roses: a sweet-smelling Albertine tumbles over the porch. There's an honest simplicity about the garden: simple straight-edged lawns, dotted with an occasional gnarled apple or lilac tree. And in winter, the jasmine's yellow-sunshine brightness contrasts with the dull pink Borsetshire brick walls.

It is just as one would expect indoors, too: the low-beamed chintzy sitting-room, coolly welcoming on a warm summer's evening. The homely simplicity of bowls of full-blown peonies, dropping their petals on the faded sill. Winter-time will woo you with crackling log fires on Sunday afternoons. The peacefully ticking longcase clock promises treats of hot buttery toast and steaming Earl Grey tea.

Brookfield has been a haven and a sanctuary for me ever since my childhood. With my satchel bumping on my back, my sandalled feet would race along the dusty lane from school to impart some news to my plump, homely grandmother, busy in the kitchen. She was the great comforter, the curer of all ills and the giver of much happiness. I would sit up to the scrubbed-top wooden table, a slice of freshly baked bread spread thickly with salty farmhouse butter put in front of me, and talk. So you can understand why the farm meant – and still means – so much to me. It has the feel of a living being with a soul and a pulse. And its enveloping atmosphere

makes it more than just a house and home.

Brookfield Farm has changed little over the years. No longer Dan and Doris living there, but their son Phil and his wife Jill, now the matriarch, the doer of good, the one we all admire for her equable spirit, her diligence and devotion to her family. Phil will stay on just as long as his hips will allow, with David and Ruth as part of the farming team. They live no distance away in a square, squat, purpose-built bungalow on Brookfield land.

It is no wonder that Jill has a steady stream of 'townies' queuing for her B & B farm holidays – much to Phil's aggravation! After all, who enjoys having to wait for the bathroom, or having one's beloved piano thumped on by children's sticky fingers? However, all this is in the cause of that frightful *farming term 'diversification'. I never cease to be amazed by Jill's competence. However does she find the time to cope with meals-on-wheels, to keep her bees, to prune her roses and cook such good wholesome farmhouse food? No boil-in-the-bag bourguignon for her! The stockpot is replenished regularly; ham bones are never wasted; soil-encrusted vegetables are dug fresh from the garden, with the occasional help from Bert Fry. There are always free-range eggs to feature in fluffy omelettes and smooth, sweet honey to spread on spicy scones.*

So this is where we go next on our culinary expedition around the village of Ambridge. I'll step inside the porch now, tug off my wellies, hang my Barbour on the peg and grab a clean tea towel – there are plenty on the front of the Aga – and help dry up while Jill tells me all about Christmas dinner at Brookfield.

Christmas wouldn't be Christmas if the Archer family wasn't gathered together under the beamed Brookfield ceilings to celebrate the season and share in the fare. It is still just as it was in Dan and Doris's day: church in the morning while the turkey slowly roasts in the Aga; then fires are lit, the family arrives, presents are opened round the tree and all settle down to a traditional Christmas dinner.

LEMONY FORCEMEAT STUFFING

12oz (350g) white breadcrumbs
4tbsp chopped fresh herbs (marjoram, thyme, sage)
or 2tsp dried herbs
6tbsp chopped parsley
salt and pepper
grated rind and juice of 1 small lemon
6oz (175g) butter
3 medium size eggs

Mix together the breadcrumbs, herbs, chopped parsley, seasoning and grated lemon rind.

Melt the butter, mix the eggs and lemon juice and bind all the ingredients together to make a moist stuffing. This is enough to stuff the breast of a 12–14lb (5.5–6.5kg) turkey.

CHESTNUT AND CELERY STUFFING

2lb (1kg) chestnuts
6 sticks celery
4oz (100g) soaked dried apricots
4oz (100g) white breadcrumbs
1tbsp chopped parsley
salt and freshly milled pepper
1 medium size egg
2oz (50g) melted butter

Slit the shells of the chestnuts, boil for 30 minutes, and shell while still hot. Press through a sieve.

Finely chop the celery and apricots. Combine with the breadcrumbs, parsley and seasoning and mix thoroughly with the beaten egg and melted butter.

This is sufficient to stuff the cavity of a plucked and drawn 12lb (5.5kg) turkey.

CRUNCHY ROAST POTATOES

These are cooked in a separate roasting tin with 2 or 3oz (50–75g) melted cooking fat.

First parboil the potatoes for 4–5 minutes. Drain, then score the surface of the potatoes with a fork. For golden-brown, crisp potatoes, roast in the cooking fat in a roasting tin near the top of a hot oven 425°F/220°C/Gas 7 for about an hour, turning occasionally.

CRANBERRY AND ORANGE SAUCE

This can be put through a sieve or blender if a smoother sauce is preferred.

1lb (450g) fresh cranberries
5fl oz (150ml/¼pt) orange juice
1 cinnamon stick
6oz (175g) granulated sugar
grated zest of 1 orange

Put the cranberries in a saucepan with the orange juice and the cinnamon stick and bring slowly to the boil. Simmer gently. When the skins begin to pop, remove from the heat and stir in the sugar and the orange zest.

BRUSSELS SPROUTS WITH PINE NUTS

Prepare the sprouts by cutting off the outside leaves. Boil them in salted water in a lidded pan for 8–10 minutes, then drain well.

Place the pine nuts in a pan with melted butter and fry until brown. Pour the butter and nuts over the hot brussels sprouts and then serve immediately.

CREAMED CELERIAC

SERVES 4–6

This is a smooth and creamy dish with a pronounced celery flavour. You may prefer freshly ground black pepper to the nutmeg or mace.

2lb (1kg) celeriac root
4oz (100g) unsalted butter
5fl oz (150ml/¼pt) double cream
2tsp caster sugar
½tsp grated nutmeg or mace

Peel the celeriac, cut into large chunks and place in a saucepan. Boil in salted water until tender. Drain well, then return to the pan to dry over a very low heat. Mash thoroughly, or purée in a blender or food processor.

Melt the butter in a pan over a low heat, add the mashed or puréed vegetable, the cream, sugar and seasoning. Keep stirring until the purée is well mixed and piping hot.

COUNTRY · CUTTINGS

Jill says, 'Carrots and dried apricots, boiled together then puréed and seasoned with mace, make a good smooth sauce to accompany roast loin of pork.'

When pouring flaming brandy over a Christmas pudding put sugar on top.

CHRISTMAS PUDDING

MAKES 2 PUDDINGS: 1½ AND 1PT

Jill Archer's special rich Christmas pudding recipe, handed down from the Forrest family, has been added to and improved by Jill over the years. Remember to heat the brandy or rum in a warm spoon before pouring it over the pudding and lighting it.

4 dessert apples, peeled and finely chopped
8oz (225g) sultanas
8oz (225g) raisins
8oz (225g) currants
2oz (50g) chopped mixed peel
2oz (50g) glacé cherries
the best part of ½ a 37.5cl bottle of rum
8oz (225g) self-raising flour
1oz (25g) ground ginger
1tsp mixed spice
8oz (225g) shredded suet
4oz (100g) soft brown sugar
2oz (50g) ground almonds
1oz (25g) flaked almonds
14oz (400g) fresh white breadcrumbs
2 medium size eggs
juice of 1 orange
juice of 1 lemon
30fl oz (900ml/1½pt) (approximately) old ale

Assemble all the fruit in a large bowl and soak generously in rum. Leave in a cool place overnight, covered with a cloth.

Sieve the flour and spices together and add the suet, sugar, ground and flaked almonds and breadcrumbs. Mix all these dry ingredients into the fruit.

Beat the eggs in a separate basin, together with the fruit juices and remaining rum before adding to the fruit mixture. Finally add the old ale, mixing thoroughly to obtain a 'loose batter' consistency. Cover with a cloth and leave overnight.

The next day divide the mixture into two basins, cover with a double thickness of greaseproof paper and steam for up to 10 hours. The longer the steaming the darker the puddings will be. Remember to keep topping up the water.

Cool and replace the covers.

On Christmas Day, steam briskly for 2 hours and then serve with brandy butter.

BRANDY BUTTER

SERVES 12

6oz (175g) unsalted butter
8oz (225g) icing sugar
zest of 1 small orange
2tbsp brandy

Cream the butter and sifted icing sugar together and add the orange zest. Beat in the brandy and chill before serving.

CHUNKY CHRISTMAS CRUNCH

SERVES 6 AT LEAST

A wickedly rich concoction for chocolate lovers – even more so when served with cream. Nigel's favourite.

8oz (225g) butter
2tbsp golden syrup
8oz (225g) good quality dark chocolate
1tbsp cocoa powder
1tbsp rum
8oz (225g) plain sweet biscuits, crushed
6oz (175g) Uncle Walter's ginger nuts, crushed
2oz (50g) preserved ginger, chopped
2oz (50g) glacé cherries, halved
2oz (50g) walnut pieces, chopped
a sprig of holly

Melt the butter, syrup and chocolate in a saucepan over a low heat. Stir in the cocoa and rum, then add the crushed biscuits, ginger pieces, cherries and chopped walnuts.

Spoon the mixture into a greased 2pt pudding basin, pressing down well. Chill in a fridge to harden, dipping the basin in hot water before turning out. Decorate with a colourful sprig of holly.

BRANDY WAFERS

MAKES ABOUT 20

Jill usually offers these to accompany her Lemon Boodles Fool.

4oz (100g) butter
4oz (100g) demerara sugar
4oz (100g) golden syrup
2tsp brandy
4oz (100g) plain flour
1tsp (level) ground ginger
1tsp (level) cinnamon

In a saucepan warm the butter, sugar and syrup together gently on a low heat. When the butter has melted add the brandy. Sift in the flour, together with the cinnamon and ginger and mix well.

Drop teaspoonfuls of the mixture on to a greased baking tray, leaving plenty of room for them to spread. Bake for 10 minutes at 350°F/180°C/Gas 4.

Leave to cool for a minute or so, then roll up each biscuit around the handle of a wooden spoon. Cool on a wire tray.

LEMON BOODLES FOOL

SERVES 6–8

A light, tangy and refreshing alternative to the rich Christmas puddings.

24 sponge finger biscuits
10fl oz (275ml/½pt) double cream
10fl oz (275ml/½pt) Greek yogurt
juice and grated rind of 4 oranges and 2 lemons
2tbsp caster sugar

Crumble twelve of the sponge fingers into the base of a glass bowl.

Put the cream into a large mixing bowl with the grated orange and lemon rind. Squeeze the juice from the fruit, sieve it and stir in the sugar until dissolved.

Whip the cream and the yogurt together, slowly adding the fruit juice. Pour half of this whipped cream mixture on to the sponge fingers, add the remaining crumbled sponge fingers and top with the rest of the cream. Chill in the fridge for several hours before serving.

A little finely grated lemon peel to garnish adds an extra zest.

MULLED WINE

When the carol singers arrive from St Stephen's on a cold and frosty evening before Christmas they will certainly be welcomed by Phil and Jill with mulled wine and mince pies.

6oz (175g) caster sugar
½ 75cl bottle water
2 75cl bottles red wine
1 lemon stuck with 6 cloves
1in piece of fresh root ginger
thinly pared rind of 1 orange
1 cinnamon stick
juice of 2 lemons

Measure the sugar and water into a saucepan and stir over a low heat until the sugar has dissolved. Add the wine and the rest of the ingredients and heat gently until steaming.

Remove from the heat, cover and allow to stand for 10 minutes. Remove the cinnamon, lemon, ginger and cloves, but leave the orange rind to float in the wine. Pour into a warmed punch bowl.

MINCEMEAT

MAKES ABOUT 5LB

There's a bit of an argument as to whether this is Doris's recipe or Auntie Pru's, but it's jolly good whoever first made it!

1lb (450g) cooking apples
4oz (100g) candied peel
4oz (100g) blanched almonds
8oz (225g) dried apricots
1lb (450g) shredded suet
8oz (225g) stoned raisins
8oz (225g) sultanas
4oz (100g) chopped glacé cherries
1lb (450g) soft brown sugar
1tsp cinnamon
10fl oz (275ml/ ½pt) ginger wine
1 small wine glass brandy
grated rind and juice of 2 lemons

Peel, core and chop the apples. Chop the peel, nuts and dried apricots.

Place these and all the remaining ingredients in a large bowl, and mix well. The mincemeat can be stored in an earthenware jar with a well-fitting lid, or put into individual covered jars. Use within one month.

MINCE PIES

MAKES 16 PIES

This pastry recipe of Jill's makes the mince pies crumbly and deliciously moreish.

After baking, to make them even more special, a dollop of cream cheese mixed with grated orange zest can be popped under each pastry lid.

Heat them again before serving.

8oz (225g) plain flour
pinch of salt
5oz (150g) butter
2oz (50g) ground almonds
4oz (100g) caster sugar
grated rind of ½ lemon
1 medium size egg beaten
1lb (450g) Jill's special mincemeat

Sieve together the flour and salt and rub in the butter until it resembles fine breadcrumbs. Stir in the ground almonds, sugar and lemon rind and bind together with the beaten egg. Chill for 30 minutes before using.

Roll the pastry out to ¼in thick, and cut out bases and lids to fit greased patty tins. Place 1tsp of mincemeat in each base, and top with a dampened pastry lid. Prick each pie with a fork and bake for 25–30 minutes near the top of a hot oven (400°F/200°C/Gas 6) until golden brown.

Doris always applied camphor dissolved in paraffin to rid furniture of woodworm.

SIMNEL CAKE

The traditional Easter tea table isn't complete without Brookfield's Simnel Cake, usually decorated with eleven marzipan balls. However this year speckled sugar eggs are in pride of place!

FOR THE ALMOND PASTE
6oz (175g) caster sugar
6oz (175g) sifted icing sugar
12oz (350g) ground almonds
2 medium size eggs
1tsp lemon juice

FOR THE CAKE
6oz (175g) butter
6oz (175g) soft brown sugar
3 medium size eggs
grated rind of 1 lemon
grated rind of 1 orange
8oz (225g) plain flour
1tsp baking powder
¼ tsp grated nutmeg
¼ tsp cinnamon
salt
1lb (450g) mixed dried fruit
2oz (50g) glacé cherries
1tbsp milk

To make the paste, combine the sugars with the ground almonds. Add the beaten egg and lemon juice. Work together well and roll out.

Grease and line a 7in cake tin.

Cream the butter and sugar, gradually adding the eggs and the grated lemon and orange rind. Sieve the flour and baking powder and add with the spices. Add the dried fruit, halved cherries and milk, and mix well.

Place half the mixture in the lined tin, smooth the top and cover with a round of almond paste. Add the remaining cake mixture and bake for 2¼–3 hours at 325°F/160°C/Gas 3.

When cold, cover the top of the cake with a round of almond paste. Decorate with sugared eggs or marzipan balls and tie a yellow ribbon round the cake.

COUNTRY·CUTTINGS

Jill makes an easy sweet sauce for puddings by mixing together, over a low heat, the juice and grated rind of an orange and a lemon, ½ teacup of runny honey and a beaten egg, stirring till it thickens.

EASTER BISCUITS

MAKES 24

These traditional Easter biscuits are always tied together in threes to represent the Trinity.

5oz (150g) butter or margarine
5oz (150g) caster sugar
1 medium size egg
8oz (225g) plain flour
a pinch of cinnamon
2oz (50g) currants
1oz (25g) candied peel

Cream the butter and sugar and add the beaten egg. Stir in the sifted flour and cinnamon, currants and candied peel.

Roll out ¼in thick and cut out the biscuits with a fluted cutter. Cook on a baking tray for about 20 minutes at 400°F/200°C/Gas 6 until lightly coloured. Sprinkle with a little caster sugar.

HOT CROSS BUNS

MAKES 12

There's nothing quite like the warm cinnamony smell of Jill's hot cross buns baking in the Aga at Brookfield. A real Easter treat!

1lb (450g) plain flour
1tsp salt
1tsp ground cinnamon
1tsp mixed spice
2oz (50g) butter
2tbsp caster sugar
2oz (50g) currants
1oz (25g) candied peel
1oz (25g) fresh yeast
about 10fl oz (275ml/½pt) milk
1 medium size egg

Sieve the flour with the salt and spices into a large bowl. Rub in the butter and add the sugar (saving a little for the yeast), currants and candied peel.

Cream the yeast with the remaining sugar and add the tepid milk. Pour into the centre of the flour and leave to sponge for about 10 minutes, then mix to a dough with the beaten egg.

Cover the bowl with a clean tea towel and leave in a warm place for the dough to rise. When it has doubled its size, turn on to a floured board, knead well and divide into twelve portions. Roll each into a flattened ball shape. Cut a deep cross on each one and place on a floured baking tray. Leave to prove for about 20 minutes, then bake in a hot oven 400°F/200°C/Gas 6 for about 20 minutes.

Brush the buns with a light glaze made by dissolving a little sugar in water.

MUESLI

Sweetened with the honey from Brookfield's own hives, this makes a fresh and healthy start to the day. Phil isn't too sure about it, but it's a great favourite of Elizabeth's and Jill's bed-and-breakfast guests.

This recipe should be enough for 4 servings.

4tbsp porridge oats
approximately 10fl oz (275ml/½pt) water
3tbsp thick, whole milk yogurt
1–2tbsp honey
juice of ½ lemon
3–4 dessert apples
1tbsp ground or chopped hazelnuts

Soak the oats in almost 10fl oz (275ml/½pt) water overnight.

The next morning stir in the yogurt, honey and lemon juice. Grate the unpeeled apples and stir these in. Add the chopped nuts, and serve.

COUNTRY · CUTTINGS

Jill says, always remember to prick the shell of an egg to prevent it from bursting when being boiled.

KEDGEREE

SERVES 4–6

Jill's kedgeree makes a delicious breakfast alternative to bacon and eggs, or sausage and mushrooms. She prefers to use kipper fillets rather than the conventional smoked haddock, and always sprinkles on lots of freshly chopped parsley before serving.

8oz (225g) kipper fillets
8oz (225g) rice
2oz (50g) butter
1 medium onion, chopped
4 hard-boiled eggs
1tsp lemon juice
5fl oz (150ml/¼pt) single cream
1tsp chopped parsley
1 pinch cayenne pepper
salt and freshly ground black pepper

Cover the kipper fillets in cold water and poach for about 10 minutes, then flake the kippers from skin and bone.

Simmer the rice in plenty of lightly salted water until soft but not soggy.

Melt the butter in a large saucepan, add the onion and cook over a low heat until transparent. Stir in the cooked rice, chopped hard-boiled eggs, flaked fish, and lemon juice.

Heat through, then add the cream, chopped parsley, and adjust the seasoning.

WHOLEMEAL SCONES

MAKES 10–12

These are delicious at tea time with Brookfield honey, or at breakfast with marmalade, but are at their very best eaten warm straight from the oven, and spread thickly with butter!

4oz (100g) plain flour
4oz (100g) wholemeal flour
1tsp bicarbonate of soda
pinch salt
2tsp cream of tartar
1½oz (40g) butter
2oz (50g) sultanas
¼tsp cinnamon
¼tsp powdered nutmeg
1 medium size egg
4tbsp milk, to mix

Sift the flours, bicarbonate of soda, salt and cream of tartar into a bowl – adding the bran left over in the sieve. Rub in the butter until the mixture resembles fine breadcrumbs. Stir in the sultanas, cinnamon and nutmeg.

Add the beaten egg to the milk and pour this into the centre of the flour mixture. Using the blade of a knife, mix into a rough dough. Knead lightly, then turn on to a floured surface and roll out until ½in thick. Using a 1½in or 2in pastry cutter, stamp out the scones.

Put on greased baking trays and place in a hot oven at 425°F/220°C/Gas 7 for 10–15 minutes – or until well risen.

BONFIRE PARTY

'D'YOU REMEMBER THAT SAYING, the one that Phil's always quoting about the sparks flying upward?' Brian and I, Barboured and booted, sat in the comparative comfort of the Range Rover. Behind us were boxes of savoury baked-in-the-Aga potatoes donated by my not-usually-so-generous brother, Tony.

Outside, eager villagers in quilted coats and anoraks were bunched together in groups with much stamping of feet and blowing on cold fingers.

The fields had turned from gold to brown; the fretwork of trees was silhouetted against the grey skies, and the sun hung like a feeble lantern trying in vain to prolong the short afternoon. It was no fun; it was November.

For some weeks twigs, branches, sticks and boxes had been piling up Grundy-fashion in a growing stack on the village green. Snooping Lynda Snell had taken it upon herself to poke and prod and hopefully disturb any unsuspecting hibernating hedgehog. As the mound grew so did the excitement of the local children – and the local children's mothers, who organized themselves into delegating and distributing responsibilities – and lists: Ruth Archer – ginger parkin; Susan Carter – toffee apples; Sharon Richards – the guy.

A bothersome bunch of bikers swung and swerved their shining machines annoyingly close to the crowd – then roared away in the direction of Darrington, much to Kate's disappointment.

A breeze blew up – the bonfire hissed and crackled as flames leapt against the black velvet night. The spicy smell of woodsmoke wafted towards us on the cold air. Eyes shone brightly in rosy faces

glowing in the firelight. There were 'oohs' and 'aahs' as Catherine-wheels whirled and sparklers sparkled, whoops and squeaks as rockets exploded in myriads of shimmering coloured stars. Sticky lips were licked, gooey toffee was sucked and chewed and steaming hot potatoes huffed and puffed on.

The plump, misshapen figure of the guy was propped aloft, his sad, dejected form unnervingly familiar. Flames leapt around his straw-stuffed jeans, his jacket smouldered slowly. The freakish features of his face on a stuffed stocking mask melted and twisted to a ghoulish grin. Then as the fire engulfed him in a flaming orange furnace, he slumped forward in submission and showers of yellow sparks shot up into the sky. The crowd hooted and cheered – all but one – Susan (Horrobin) Carter. Then I remembered. 'Men are born to trouble as the sparks fly upward.' Poor Clive!

HOME FARM BAKED POTATOES WITH SAVOURY BUTTERS

Scrub baking-sized potatoes and cut a cross on each one. Prick the skins, rub with coarse sea salt and olive oil and wrap each potato in kitchen foil. Cook in a preheated oven at 425°F/220°C/ Gas 7 for 1½ hours.

When completely cooked open up the foil and serve with a choice of savoury butters. The following butters can be made a few hours beforehand and stored in the refrigerator. Allow 1oz (25g) butter per person.

HERBED BUTTER

SERVES 4

4oz (100g) softened butter
2tsp finely chopped parsley
1tsp chopped coriander
salt and pepper
a pinch of cayenne pepper

Pound the butter together with the herbs and seasoning until thoroughly mixed. Then chill in a covered container until needed.

BLUE CHEESE BUTTER

4oz (100g) butter
2oz (50g) Roquefort or Danish blue cheese
1 clove garlic

Pound the butter together with the cheese and garlic until thoroughly mixed. Then chill in a covered container until needed.

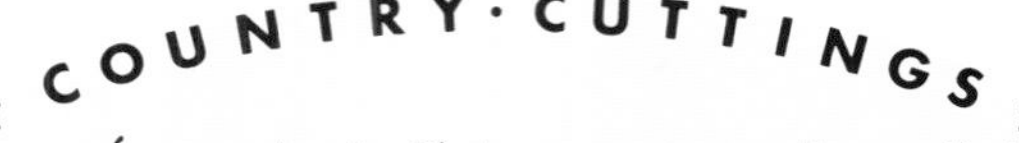

Auntie Chris suggests standing stuffed, baked apples on rounds of bread butter-side-up in a roasting tin while baking. The bread soaks up the juice and turns brown, tasting deliciously of toffee.

MUSTARD AND HORSERADISH BUTTER

4oz (100g) butter
2tsp coarse grain mustard
2tsp horseradish sauce

Pound the butter together with the mustard and horseradish sauce until thoroughly mixed. Then chill in a covered container until needed.

TOFFEE APPLES

I'm afraid Alice and her woollen mittens have discovered that if these are left in the open air too long they become very, very sticky!

12 medium size eating apples
6oz (175g) syrup
12oz (350g) demerara sugar
1oz (25g) butter
5fl oz (150ml/ ¼pt) water
1tsp vinegar
12 thin wooden sticks or skewers

Rub a baking tray with oil for the apples to stand on while they are setting. Wipe the apples, remove the stalks and insert a stick through the stalk end.

Put all the other ingredients in a heavy-based large pan and place on a low heat. Stir until all the sugar has dissolved, then bring to the boil and boil rapidly without stirring until a drop placed in cold water goes hard and snaps.

Take the pan off the heat and dip the apples in, one at a time, turning to coat evenly, then plunge into cold water. Leave to set on the greased tray.

BONFIRE TOFFEE

MAKES ABOUT 1½LB

Debbie made this sweet, bubbling recipe on the Aga at Home Farm. It played havoc with Freda Fry's dentures!

12oz (350g) soft brown sugar
5oz (150g) butter
2tbsp syrup
2½fl oz (75ml/⅛pt) water

Put all the ingredients in a heavy-based saucepan and bring slowly to the boil. After the sugar has dissolved, boil steadily until a temperature of 290°F/140°C is reached on a sugar thermometer, or until a drop of toffee forms brittle threads when placed into a cup of cold water.

Pour into a greased tin, and mark into squares with a knife before completely set.

When cold, pack in an airtight container.

GINGER PARKIN

This is Ruth's recipe, gleaned from her relations in the north. For those with a sweet tooth it can be glazed with a layer of ginger icing.

10oz (275g) wholewheat or white self-raising flour
5oz (150g) coarse oatmeal
4oz (100g) demerara sugar
1tsp bicarbonate of soda
1tsp (heaped) ground ginger
1tsp allspice
4oz (100g) syrup or treacle
3oz (75g) lard
3oz (75g) margarine
a little milk

Mix the dry ingredients together in a bowl.

In a saucepan melt the lard, margarine and syrup and stir into the dry ingredients. Stir until well mixed, adding enough milk to make a soft consistency.

Grease and line a 9in square baking tin. Put the mixture in and bake in a moderate oven at 350°F/180°C/Gas 4 for about 1 hour, or until firm. Allow to cool before turning out.

This can be stored for up to a week in an airtight container before eating.

COUNTRY · CUTTINGS

Mrs Turvey's soothing treacle posset – Heat 10fl oz (275ml/½pt) milk with 1tbsp black treacle and the juice of a lemon. Boil until the mixture separates. Sieve and serve as a warm soothing night-time drink for coughs and colds.

THE BULL

'TIME GENTLEMEN, P-LEASE'. *There was a hint of a sigh in Sid Perks' sturdy voice. Slide the bolts, hang up the towels, switch off the lights – and switch off your smile. It must be a nightmare smiling all day.*

Black and white, 'The Bull on the old village green offers home-from-home comfort and home-made food for all our customers . . .' who sit sipping pints of Shires and crunching pork scratchings in the snug, or enjoying a cheese and pickle ploughman's in the log-fired bars for the public . . . and the ploughmen!

The darts team meets the opposition from the neighbouring Cat and Fiddle, and there's National Farmers' fun in their Union members' function once a month.

And it's in this jolly, noisy pub I spent my childhood, lying awake beneath the dark-beamed ceilings above the revellers. Shrill voices carried through open windows, along with wafts of post-war Woodbines and the chink of glasses.

I clearly remember Dad leaning on the polished counter, beaming with beneficence. But, behind those smoothly swinging doors, he also leaned heavily on Mum, afflicted by his addiction to drink. As a publican he had no privacy, his private life was in the public eye. Even sparky, cheery Kathy Perks fluttered moth-like towards the light of an affair while Sid was wedded to his job – polishing the glasses, polishing the brasses and polishing his smile.

With karaoke clearly in his mind, he hoists a box of rattling bottles on to the bar, clears his throat and bursts forth in stentorian tone. 'Smile though your feet are aching, smile though your back is breaking, smile . . .'

LUCY'S VEGETABLE LASAGNE

SERVES 4

It was Lucy Perks who insisted Kathy should put some healthy vegetarian dishes on the menu at the Bull. Aubergine adds an interesting 'meaty' texture and perhaps a tablespoon of tomato purée would liven up the colour of the vegetable sauce.

1 medium aubergine
4tbsp olive oil
1 large onion, chopped
1 garlic clove, crushed
1tbsp parsley, finely chopped
1tbsp marjoram or oregano, chopped (or ¼tsp dried)
2 small courgettes, sliced
1 tin chopped tomatoes
4oz (100g) mushrooms, sliced
salt and pepper
6oz (175g) lasagne (the sort that doesn't need pre-cooking)

FOR THE SAUCE
2oz (50g) butter
2oz (50g) plain flour
20fl oz (600ml/1pt) milk
4oz (100g) grated cheese (Borset or Cheddar)
2oz (50g) parmesan
black pepper and salt
grated nutmeg

Trim the ends off the aubergine but don't peel it. Cut into ½in cubes.

Heat the oil in a large frying pan and cook the onion, garlic and herbs for 1 minute. Add the cubed aubergine and sliced courgettes and cook for a further 3–4 minutes, stirring occasionally. Add the tomatoes, mushrooms and seasoning, then cover and simmer for 20 minutes.

To make the sauce, put the butter, flour and milk into a saucepan and whisk over a moderate heat until the sauce has come to the boil and thickened.

Add the grated cheese, nutmeg, salt and black pepper.

Assemble the lasagne by first putting a layer of the vegetable mixture in the bottom of an ovenproof dish, followed by a layer of lasagne sheets. Continue with alternate layers, ending with a layer of lasagne. Top this with the sauce and sprinkle with the finely grated parmesan.

Cover with foil and bake in a preheated oven at 400°F/200°C/Gas 6 for 40 minutes, removing the foil for the last 15 minutes.

WARMING WINTER SOUP

SERVES 6

Joe eyed the floating bread with suspicion. 'They're not servin' bloomin' French muck here as well, are they? It's bad enough at 'ome.'

2oz (50g) butter
1½lb (675g) onions, thinly sliced
3 cloves garlic, chopped
2tsp sugar
8oz (225g) potatoes, diced
40fl oz (1.2L/2pt) beef stock (or 2 tins consommé)
salt and pepper
½ stick of French bread
2oz (50g) Gruyère cheese, grated

Melt the butter in a saucepan, add the onions, garlic and sugar and cook gently until the onions have browned. Add the potatoes, stock and seasoning. Bring to the boil and simmer for 15–20 minutes. Slice the bread and toast on one side.

Ladle the soup into earthenware bowls, float the pieces of toast on top, toasted side down, sprinkling the Gruyère cheese on top. Place under a hot grill until the cheese bubbles, or bake in a preheated oven at 325°F/ 160°C/Gas 3.

MOCHA FUDGE SLICE

Rich, dark and irresistible – definitely not for those on a diet!

6oz (175g) soft margarine
4oz (100g) caster sugar
4 medium size eggs
2oz (50g) self-raising flour
6oz (175g) drinking chocolate
1tsp coffee granules, dissolved in 1tbsp hot water

FOR THE FUDGE TOPPING
3oz (75g) hard margarine
8oz (225g) icing sugar
2oz (50g) cocoa
2tbsp water

Cream the margarine and sugar together until light and fluffy and beat in the eggs one by one. Beat in the sifted flour and drinking chocolate and mix well. Add the dissolved coffee and beat thoroughly.

Spoon the mixture into two greased and lined 8in sandwich tins or one large one. Bake in a preheated moderate oven at 350°F/180°C/Gas 4 for about 20–25 minutes, until well risen and firm to the touch and beginning to shrink away from the sides of the tins. Leave to cool in the tins.

To make the fudge topping, melt the margarine in a saucepan, add the sifted icing sugar and cocoa and cook for 1 minute, then beat until smooth and shiny.

Cool slightly, and then pour on to the cake, still in the tins. The fudge mixture will spread over the top of the cake and cool with a shiny surface.

Serve in slices with cream, ice-cream or yogurt.

BLACKCURRANT CHEESECAKE

Cheesecake is still a yawningly popular choice on The Bull's menu. Kathy knows how to woo her customers!

4oz (100g) digestive biscuits
2oz (50g) unsalted butter, melted
1tbsp gelatine, soaked in 3tbsp water
6oz (175g) blackcurrants
4oz (100g) cream cheese
4fl oz (100ml) thick yogurt
3oz (75g) caster sugar
5fl oz (150ml/ ¼pt) double cream, lightly whipped

Crush the biscuits and combine with the melted butter. Press the mixture into the base of an 8in loose-bottomed cake tin.

Place the gelatine in a pan with the water and heat gently.

Heat the blackcurrants in a pan and simmer in a little water until soft, then allow to cool.

Put the cream cheese, yogurt and sugar into a blender or food processor and mix thoroughly. Fold the gelatine, soft fruit and whipped cream into this mixture.

Spoon on to the biscuit base and chill until set. Remove from the cake tin, and decorate.

COURGETTE AND CELERY SOUP

SERVES 6

A late summer soup – equally good hot or cold.

8oz (225g) courgettes
1oz (25g) butter
3 celery sticks, trimmed and chopped
2 leeks, cleaned, trimmed and cut into ¼in slices
1 large onion, chopped
1oz (25g) plain flour
40fl oz (1.2L/2pt) chicken stock (or use a stock cube)
2tbsp dry sherry
4fl oz (100ml) double cream
salt and black pepper

Dice the topped and tailed courgettes. Melt the butter in a large saucepan over a moderate heat and fry the celery, leeks and onion until they have softened.

When the onion becomes transparent stir in the flour to make a paste. Gradually add the stock and sherry, stirring all the time. Add the diced courgettes, bring to the boil and simmer for 20 minutes.

Purée in a blender or food processor and then stir in the double cream. Add salt and pepper to taste.

TRAWLERMAN'S PIE

SERVES 4

Kathy sometimes adds a layer of quartered hard-boiled eggs before the potato is spread over the top. The cheese can be mixed together with the creamy mashed potato if preferred.

1½lb (675g) cod fillet
15fl oz (425ml/ ¾pt) milk
1½oz (40g) butter
1 small onion, chopped
2tbsp chopped celery
1½oz (40g) flour
4oz (100g) mushrooms, sliced
2tbsp chopped parsley
2tsp anchovy essence
salt and pepper
5fl oz (150ml/ ¼pt) single cream
1lb (450g) potatoes, boiled and mashed
3oz (75g) grated cheese

Put the fish in a saucepan, cover with the milk and poach for 10 minutes. When cooked, take out the fish, remove any skin and bones, and reserve the liquid.

Heat the butter in a saucepan and add the chopped onion and celery and fry until tender. Blend in the flour and stir to make a roux. Add

the reserved milk and blend together to make a smooth sauce. Bring to the boil and simmer for 2 minutes. Add the sliced mushrooms, chopped parsley, anchovy essence, seasoning and cream. Add the flaked fish to the sauce and pour into an ovenproof dish. Cover with the mashed potato and sprinkle with grated cheese.

Bake in a preheated oven at 375°F/190°C/Gas 5 for about 20 minutes, until the top is golden.

SMOKED MACKEREL PÂTÉ

SERVES 6–8

A very special pâté when made with Auntie Pru's home-made horseradish cream.

3 large smoked mackerel
12oz (350g) curd cheese
1tbsp chopped parsley
finely grated rind and juice of 1 lemon
1oz (25g) softened butter
2tbsp horseradish cream
pepper and salt

Remove the skin and bones from the cooked mackerel. Add the cheese and mix thoroughly by hand or in a blender or food processor.

Add the chopped parsley, lemon rind and juice, softened butter, horseradish cream and seasoning. Blend or stir the mixture thoroughly.

Pack into ramekin dishes or a large mould. Cover and refrigerate until required, but keep for two days at most.

Serve with hot toast and wedges of lemon.

COUNTRY · CUTTINGS

Sprinkle a little caster sugar on tomatoes before grilling.

Sprinkle sugar on custard to prevent a skin forming.

LEMON GINGER CHICKEN

SERVES 8

Much, much better than dull 'chicken in a basket', this also goes well with rice.

8 chicken joints, skinned
2oz (50g) plain flour
2tbsp olive oil
a knob of butter
1 large onion, chopped
1 green pepper, deseeded and chopped
1 clove garlic, crushed
1in piece of fresh root ginger, peeled and finely chopped
4oz (100g) mushrooms, sliced
grated rind of 1 lemon
10fl oz (275ml/ ½pt) dry white wine

Dust the chicken joints in flour. Heat the oil and butter in a large frying pan and fry the joints until browned. Transfer them to an ovenproof dish.

Put the onion and green pepper into the pan and sauté for a few minutes. Add the garlic, ginger, mushrooms and lemon rind and then gradually stir in the wine. Bring to the boil and pour the vegetable mixture over the chicken.

Place in a medium oven at 375°F/190°C/Gas 5 for 30–40 minutes.

Serve with a crisp green salad and French bread.

Brownies' Summer Picnic

'Take that road out of the village, the one towards Borchester. And don't forget, look up to your right when you've passed the Green and you can't miss it.'

Lakey Hill, brown and ridged on one side, speckled with heather and studded with gorse on the other. It's not particularly dramatic, but the gently rising slopes hold so many secrets. Underneath its furrowed earth, Bronze Age mysteries are hidden. Up that sandy path villagers have trod for centuries, the wind whistling in their ears and stinging their eyes on winter afternoons. They have felt, too, the heady warmth of summer days, the drone of bees softening their brows and soothing their sorrows.

It was here I walked when worry wouldn't let me sleep, pregnant with my first child Adam, whose father didn't even know. A quarter of a century later, my heart thumping with borrowed ecstasy, Roger and I gazed out from here into the misty distance, away from the village and from reality, to the space between South Borsetshire and the grey hills of obscurity. A transient happiness.

Today, on a bright morning in June, the spring brilliance of hedges turning to a gentler shade of green, the yellowhammers darting, you'll see a crocodile of little legs, keen with youth's fresh anticipation of a sun-filled, fun-filled day. Bouncing bags knocking against knees, plastic carriers proclaiming 'Underwoods – The Best in Borchester', are all stuffed with gastronomic pleasures, hopefully not squashed beyond salvation. The Ambridge Brownie pack is moving towards magical, mystical Lakey Hill. Stragglers, last to climb the splintery wooden stile are chided. 'Buck up, Becky, we haven't got all day!' But they had. A day that unfurled with simple, wholesome, tumbling fun.

'Run and find some "eggs and bacon", buttercups and "granny's bonnets",' Brown Owl hooted. 'First back to the Toadstool earns five points. Well done Emma! Five for the Finches . . .'

Later, as the damp shadows stretch across the eastern side of the hill, the weary tawny team descends the grassy slopes. Those plimsolled feet of childhood plod down the path to meet the ribbon of lane that winds towards home.

PITTA PICNIC POCKETS

Warm the pitta bread in the oven before you add the fillings. Each pitta can be cut in half to make two perfect pockets, and filled with your favourite sandwich fillings:

Tuna, mayonnaise and avocado.
Hard-boiled egg mashed with apricot chutney.
Sardines combined with cream cheese and snipped chives.
Taramasalata and prawns with chopped parsley.
Chopped cooked chicken combined with cream, Dijon mustard and a hint of curry powder.

All of these are packed together with crisp lettuce leaves, peppery watercress and thin slices of succulent beef tomatoes. Wrap each pitta pocket firmly in foil to keep the filling intact.

FILO PASTRY PARCELS

MAKES 12 PARCELS

Probably too sophisticated for the Grundy boys – or the Tuckers – but Susan Carter said Emma and Christopher really loved them.

3 shallots
3oz (75g) butter
10oz (275g) can asparagus spears, drained and chopped
2tbsp plain flour
10fl oz (275ml/ ½pt) milk
4oz (100g) Gruyère cheese, grated
salt and freshly ground black pepper
1 400g (14oz) box filo pastry

Slice the shallots and soften in 1oz (25g) of melted butter and cook gently for 2–3 minutes. Add the asparagus (having discarded any woody stems) and heat through. Add the flour, heat gently and then stir in the milk to make a smooth sauce. Add the grated Gruyère and season with salt and black pepper.

Melt the remaining 2oz (50g) butter in a pan. Spread out the filo pastry sheets on a clean worktop and brush the butter on them, one at a time. (The pastry dries out very quickly so keep it covered with a damp tea towel.)

Cut the pastry into 5in squares, lay three squares on top of each other, and spoon a large teaspoonful of the asparagus mixture on to the centre of each square. Gather up the corners and pinch them together to form a sealed parcel. Brush the outside of each parcel with melted butter. Place them on a buttered baking tray and bake at 375°F/190°C/Gas 5 for 10–15 minutes, until crisp and golden. Freeze any unused filo pastry.

COUNTRY · CUTTINGS

Uncle Walter's wisdom:
'A swarm of bees in May
Is worth a load of hay.
A swarm of bees in July
Is not worth a butterfly.'

Cure the tingling of nettle stings by rubbing with rosemary, sage, mint or the well-known dock leaves.

SESAME SCOTCH EGGS

Alice's podgy little hands can't wait to squash the sausage meat around the eggs. If the sesame seeds won't stick, roll the Scotch eggs in beaten egg rather than milk.

2 medium size eggs
4oz (100g) sausage meat
2tbsp sesame seeds
a little milk
a little flour

Put the eggs into a pan of cold water, bring to the boil, and boil for 10 minutes. Cool in a bowl of cold water and then remove the shells.

Divide the sausage meat into two halves and roll out each piece on a floured board.

Place one egg in the centre of each piece of sausage meat and wrap the sausage meat around it, making sure that all the joins are pinched together. Now roll each Scotch egg, first in milk and then in the sesame seeds, making sure the seeds are pressed firmly into the meat.

Wrap each one in foil and bake in the oven at 375°F/190°C/Gas 5 for 45–50 minutes.

Allow to cool and then pack in fresh foil for the picnic.

STRAWBERRY CREAM CROISSANTS

Take plenty of paper napkins or kitchen roll to mop up the oozing cream on chins and T-shirts.

4 croissants
2fl oz (50ml) double cream
2oz (50g) fromage frais
1tbsp icing sugar
2tbsp redcurrant jelly (or raspberry jam)
6oz (175g) ripe strawberries

Slice the croissants horizontally, but do not cut right through.

Whip the double cream, adding the fromage frais and the icing sugar.

Open the croissants and spread the jelly on the inside. Spoon in the cream, spreading it as evenly as possible, finally filling with sliced strawberries. Wrap each croissant in foil and chill in a refrigerator.

Transport to the picnic in a cool box if possible.

CHRISTOPHER CARTER'S CHOCOLATE CRUNCHIES

MAKES ABOUT 36 BISCUITS

'These will keep crisp for a long time in a tin or plastic box – unless Emma gets her hands on them first!' says Susan.

8oz (225g) butter or hard margarine
4oz (100g) caster sugar
1tsp vanilla essence
8oz (225g) self-raising flour
1oz (25g) cocoa
1 oz (25g) drinking chocolate

Cream together the butter and sugar with the vanilla essence until pale and fluffy.

Gradually beat in the sifted flour, cocoa and drinking chocolate.

With rinsed hands roll the mixture into spheres the size of golf balls. Then place on ungreased baking trays and flatten with a damp fork.

Bake in a moderate oven at 350°F/180°C/Gas 4 for 8–10 minutes. Transfer to a wire rack to cool.

HOME-MADE LEMON DRINK

Thirst-quenching, healthy and wholesome – everything that Kate despises!

6 lemons
2lb (1kg) granulated sugar
40fl oz (1.2L/2pt) water, boiling

Scrub the lemons and peel thinly with a sharp knife. Squeeze the juice from them and place in a jug with the sugar and lemon rind. Cover and stand in a cool place for an hour.

Slowly pour over the boiling water and allow to stand overnight. Then strain into bottles.

Keep in a cool place. Dilute to serve.

LOWER LOXLEY HALL

IT WAS JUST LYING THERE, in Richard Locke's dingy waiting room, on top of a pile of thumbed, outdated copies of Woman's Realm *and* Farmers' Weekly.

The magazine tempted me. Its glossy cover interested me. How could I ignore the majestically handsome, crumbling façade featured on the front cover of this month's Borsetshire Life? *As I thumbed I thought, and as I thought I knew . . . 'turn to page 6 for full story'.*

The article began: 'Lying deep in the lush [damp] valley of the Am, surrounded by acres of unspoilt [unkempt] parkland, stands [but only just] Lower Loxley Hall. This jewel of Jacobean architecture . . .' Of course I know – but not everybody does – that to save this historic pile from the further ravages of rot, beetle, ever-sinking foundations [and funds] . . . 'this [quasi] stately home is being opened for . . .' turn the page . . . 'rollicking, rumbustious, Elizabethan feasts'.

My mind wanders. The smoke wafts to the rafters in the galleried hall. I hear the crackling logs, the spit-roasting sucking-pigs. Pomandered wenches swing stone jars of ruby wine and courtiers, cod-pieced and farthingaled, step rhythmically to the sack-buts' mournful moan – while golden sovereigns roll and cash registers register…

Now I'm greeted by a shady, peaceful scene, the spacious landscape of an eighteenth century garden with a limpid, silvery lake and peacocks strutting on cedared lawns. 'Evenings of Baroque music in floodlit grounds by the Mellifluous Ensemble'.

I have seen Lady Henrietta (late wife of the even later Sir Rupert) looking down in abject despair on the shell-suited hoi polloi shuffling through the library beneath her pinioned portrait. I know she is thinking, 'Jousting on the lawn maybe, but gingham cloths and car parks, crisp bags and coaches (not to mention chemical conveniences) are the ghastly ideas of the stooping-lower-than-ever Lower Loxley Corporate Leisure Group!' Send for full details to Mr and Mrs Nigel Pargetter… And best of luck, I say.

☆ ELIZABETHAN FEAST MENU ☆

RICH VENISON STEW

SERVES 6

To allow the venison to develop its full flavour, Brian says it should be hung for 1–2 weeks. The marinade will moisten the meat and give it a wonderful spicy taste.

FOR THE MARINADE
1 small onion, chopped
1 celery stick, chopped
1 carrot, sliced
1 strip orange peel
4tbsp oil
5fl oz (150ml/ 1/4pt) red wine
1tsp powdered cinnamon
1tsp mace
6 whole cloves

3lb (1.5kg) boned leg or shoulder of venison, cut into 1in (25mm) cubes
2oz (50g) butter
8oz (225g) streaky bacon, chopped
2 medium onions, sliced
4tbsp plain flour
3tbsp rowan jelly
1 bouquet garni
1 bay leaf
salt and black pepper
10fl oz (275ml/1/2pt) port

Mix all the marinade ingredients together and soak the venison cubes in the mixture overnight.

Drain the venison and pat dry. Strain the marinade and reserve the liquid.

Heat the butter in a large heavy-based saucepan. Fry the bacon and onions in the butter until they are transparent. Remove to an ovenproof casserole.

Sauté the venison over a moderate heat, turning to brown evenly. Remove with a slotted spoon to the casserole.

Sprinkle the flour in the pan and add the remaining marinade, stirring all the time, including the residue from the sides of the pan. Stir in the rowan jelly.

Pour this mixture over the venison in the casserole and add the bouquet garni, bay leaf and seasoning.

Add the port, cover the casserole and place in a slow oven at 350°F/180°C/Gas 4 for 2¼–2½ hours, or until the meat is tender.

Discard the bay leaf and bouquet garni. Serve with baked potatoes and braised celery or red cabbage.

COUNTRY·CUTTINGS

A lump of sugar in the water will keep cut flowers fresh.

To crystallise grapes or edible flowers such as violets and rose petals, paint with frothy beaten egg white and dust with caster sugar. Leave to dry and harden at room temperature.

BRAISED RED CABBAGE WITH APPLES

SERVES 6–8

The smell of this piquant dish simmering on the Aga always makes me think of Christmas. The amount of sugar and vinegar can be adjusted to your liking.

1tbsp vegetable oil
1 large onion, chopped
1 medium head of red cabbage (about 1½lb/675g)
2 large cooking apples
salt and black pepper
2tbsp demerara sugar
5tbsp red wine vinegar
a little water
salt and pepper

Heat the oil in a large saucepan and cook the peeled and chopped onion until soft.

Shred the cabbage, cutting away the core. Peel, core and slice the apples and add these and the cabbage to the onion. Add the rest of the ingredients, with just enough water to prevent the cabbage sticking to the bottom of the pan.

Cover with a lid and simmer gently for about 1–1½ hours.

CLARET JELLY WITH SWEET SYLLABUB

SERVES 6–8

The clever combination of flavours and textures makes this heady dessert a triumph. I have to keep reminding Brian just how boozy it is.

FOR THE CLARET JELLY
8oz (225g) caster sugar
8fl oz (225ml/ ½pt) hot water
1fl oz (30ml) blackcurrant syrup
1oz (25g) gelatine
1tbsp brandy
20fl oz (600ml/1pt) claret

FOR THE SWEET SYLLABUB
1 lemon
10fl oz (275ml/ ½pt) white wine
1tbsp brandy
3oz (75g) caster sugar
20fl oz (600ml/1pt) double cream

To make the claret jelly, dissolve the sugar in 6fl oz (175ml) of the water in a saucepan over a low heat. Stir in the blackcurrant syrup.

Sprinkle the gelatine into the remaining 2fl oz (60ml) of water, and dissolve in a bowl over a pan of hot water. Stir until dissolved.

Stir the dissolved gelatine into the blackcurrant mixture and then add the claret and brandy.

Pour into glasses and chill until set.

To make the syllabub, pare the rind thinly from the lemon and squeeze out the juice. Place the lemon rind, juice, white wine and brandy in a large bowl and leave overnight.

Strain, then add the sugar and stir until dissolved.

Whip the double cream into the wine, bringing it up into soft peaks. Then chill.

Top each glass of claret jelly with a swirl of syllabub and serve.

LOWER LOXLEY HALL MUSICAL ☆ EVENING PICNIC MENU ☆

WATERLEY CROSS WATERCRESS SOUP

SERVES 4–6

Can't you just guess this is one of Julia's recipes? For her the glass of gin is certainly not *optional.*

3 bunches watercress
2oz (50g) butter
2 medium onions, chopped
2 medium potatoes, chopped
20fl oz (600ml/1pt) chicken stock (or use a stock cube)
20fl oz (600ml/1pt) milk
salt and pepper
1 wine glass gin (optional)
4tbsp single cream

Wash the watercress well and discard any tough stalks.

Melt the butter in a large saucepan, add the roughly chopped onion and potato and cook gently for 5 minutes. Pour on the stock and add half the watercress and salt and pepper. Bring to the boil and simmer for 20 minutes. Allow to cool and then purée in a food processor or blender until smooth. Add the remaining watercress and blend again to give a flecked appearance to the soup. Return to the pan, add the milk and reheat gently. Adjust the seasoning.

To serve chilled, add a dash of gin and stir a swirl of cream into each portion.

CHEESE AND PRAWN MOUSSES

MAKES 6

These creamy little mousses can be eaten straight from the ramekins with a small spoon or fork.

Serve with thinly sliced buttered brown bread.

½oz (15g) gelatine
2tbsp water
1 clove garlic
1tbsp lemon juice
2fl oz (60ml) dry white wine
4oz (100g) Gruyère or cheddar cheese, grated
6oz (175g) shelled prawns (fresh or frozen)
8oz (225g) cream cheese
salt, pepper and pinch cayenne pepper
5fl oz (150ml/ ¼pt) double cream
basil leaves

Dissolve the gelatine in 2tbsp water.

In a food processor or blender, blend the clove of garlic with the lemon juice and white wine. Add the grated cheese and prawns and blend until smooth. Add the cream cheese, gelatine and seasoning and blend again until well mixed.

Whip the cream until it stands in peaks, and fold into the cheese mixture.

Put into individual ramekin dishes, cover with cling film and chill.

Decorate each mousse with a basil leaf and pack carefully into a coolbox. These can be made one day in advance and kept in the refrigerator.

LOWER LOXLEY HAM LOAF WITH GREEN PEPPERCORNS

SERVES 4–6

A fashionable picnic recipe in the nineteenth century, this conjures up wicker chairs and tables in the sun, and maids with wind-blown, beribboned caps.

1lb (450g) cooked ham
4oz (100g) white breadcrumbs
1tsp (or more, according to taste) green peppercorns (the type in brine)
1tbsp finely chopped parsley
2 medium size eggs
5fl oz (150ml/ ¼pt) milk
mayonnaise for serving (optional)

Finely mince the ham (or chop in a processor) and mix with the breadcrumbs, parsley and peppercorns. Stir in the well beaten eggs and the milk.

Generously butter a 1½–2lb loaf tin. Press the mixture down into the tin and bake in a pre-heated oven at 300°F/150°C/Gas 2 for 50–60 minutes, or until set and lightly browned. Cool, then chill before slicing and serving. It will keep for 3–4 days.

If using as part of picnic fare, transport in the loaf tin.

POTATO, WALNUT AND LOVAGE SALAD

SERVES 3

A mixed leaf salad of frisée, lamb's lettuce and rocket, washed and dried, is the ideal bed on which to serve this walnut-dressed potato salad.

1lb (450g) waxy new potatoes (Pink Fir Apple or Jersey Royals are ideal)
1tbsp cider vinegar
salt, pepper and a pinch of sugar
1tbsp walnut oil
1tbsp light olive oil
1tbsp lemon juice
1tsp Dijon mustard
1tbsp chopped walnuts
1tbsp chopped lovage

Cook the cleaned, but not peeled, potatoes in boiling salted water, until just tender. Mix the salt, pepper and sugar into the vinegar, then add all the other ingredients, except the walnuts and lovage, and mix thoroughly together.

Strain the potatoes and toss in the vinaigrette while still warm.

Add the walnuts and lovage to the salad when cool.

The vinaigrette may be stored in a screw-top jar in the refrigerator for 3–4 weeks. Shake well before use.

COUNTRY · CUTTINGS

Sprinkle freshly ground black or pink peppercorns on strawberries to bring out the flavour.

Instead of rolling up the traditional brandy snaps, make clever little brandy wafer baskets by hanging each cooked, warm wafer over an up-turned cup to cool. When set, fill with a scoop of fruit sorbet and decorate with a crystallised flower.

Creamy Raspberry and Almond Tartlets

MAKES 6

Take the whipped cream and raspberries in separate containers and assemble at the picnic, serving the tartlets filled with the almond cream and topped with fresh raspberries. As part of a culinary feast, a coolbox is a must here!

4oz (100g) butter
6oz (150g) plain flour
1½oz (40g) caster sugar
1½oz (40g) ground almonds
1 egg yolk
water to mix
a few drops almond essence
10fl oz (275ml) double cream
1tbsp amaretto liqueur
1lb (450g) raspberries

Rub the butter into the flour, then add the sugar and ground almonds. Add the egg yolk and a little water with the almond essence to the dry ingredients, and mix until well amalgamated. Chill.

Roll out the pastry and line individual patty or bun tins, lining each one with foil and greasing well first. Bake blind at 375°F/190°C/Gas 5 for 10–15 minutes until they are pale biscuit colour. Cool a little before removing to a wire rack.

When cold, pack carefully into a tin or polythene container, ready for transportation.

Whip the cream, adding 1tbsp liqueur to give an almond flavour to the cream.

Nanny Pargetter's Orange Seed Cake

'Nanny always insisted we had this for nursery tea on Sundays,' confides Nigel. 'She never knew how much I hated those wretched caraway seeds.'

6oz (175g) butter
12oz (350g) caster sugar
2tsp caraway seeds
4 medium size eggs
1lb (450g) self-raising flour
grated rind and juice of 1 orange

Cream the butter and sugar together until light and fluffy and add the caraway seeds. Beat in the eggs and gradually sift in the flour. Add the orange juice and grated rind and mix to a batter-like consistency.

Place the mixture in a greased and lined 8in cake tin and bake in a preheated moderate oven at 350°F/180°C/Gas 4 for 1½–2 hours.

Leave in the tin for a few minutes before turning out on to a wire rack to cool. Store in an airtight container.

GLEBE COTTAGE

'IT'S THAT PRETTY ONE OVER THERE – look, by the church! Well, it would be, wouldn't it, by the church I mean, with a name like that!'

You must have noticed it before, when you walked down the village street, crouched like a timid mouse behind that tall, clipped hedge and flower-filled garden. Its low, brown roof dips steeply down to the brows of peeping windows. The picket gate is ajar, enticing you down the mossy cobbled path, to push your way through the clumps and spires of scented plants. Rosemary for one, the grey-green bush spelling remembrance. Memories of the time when Letty Lawson-Hope, the rich squire's daughter, left this cottage to my grandmother in her will.

'For all your help and thoughtful care, with love and endless gratitude to Doris Forrest, I bequeath this property . . .'

Dear Gran was not to know that half a century later her widowed husband, Dan, would spend his last years within the solace of these mellow walls. That he would sit and ponder on the rustic seat beneath a canopy of gnarled trees, with the sweet honeysuckle and climbing rose tumbling around the weathered wooden porch.

That air of wistfulness still lingers while woodsmoke rises from the same brick open fire, and multicoloured rugs are strewn on the same uneven floors. Let us hope the ageless charm and timeless beauty of Glebe Cottage will be preserved for ever.

CREAMY PEPPERED PORK

SERVES 2–3

Shula and Mark were given a wok for a wedding present. They discovered how useful it was to cook this quick and easy supper dish.

1lb (450g) pork fillet or tenderloin
1tsp ground ginger
½tsp cayenne pepper
2tbsp olive oil
2oz (50g) butter
1 medium onion, thinly sliced
1 red pepper, deseeded and thinly sliced
8oz (225g) button mushrooms, rinsed and quartered
6fl oz (175ml) white wine
6fl oz (175ml) double cream (or mixture of cream and Greek yogurt)
salt and pepper

Trim and slice the pork and cut into neat strips. Dust the strips evenly with the ginger and cayenne pepper.

Heat the olive oil and butter in the wok and stir-fry the onion and pepper, removing them when soft.

Reheat the oil in the wok and fry the strips of pork for 5 minutes. Add the mushrooms and white wine and cook until the fluid has reduced by half. Lower the heat and add the cream, and continue to heat gently until this thickens.

Season with salt and freshly ground black pepper and serve with noodles and a crunchy green salad.

Mrs Blossom's beeswax polish – Shred 2oz (50g) beeswax, the wax of a small white candle and 2oz (50g) plain white soap into 10fl oz (275ml/½pt) of turpentine or white spirit. Gradually add 10fl oz (275ml/½pt) of boiling water and stir thoroughly. Put into screw top jars and label carefully.

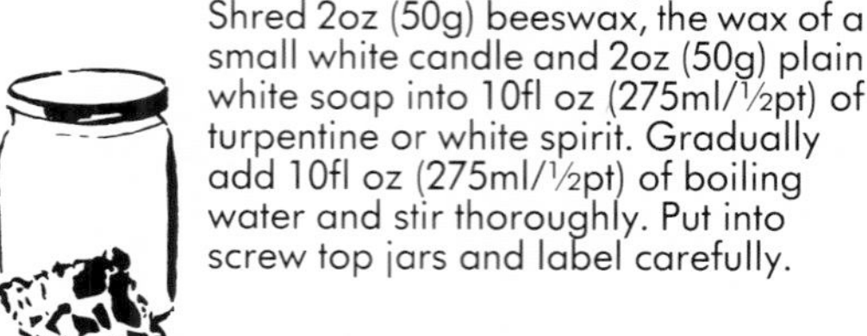

PASTA WITH TUNA, GARLIC AND SUN-DRIED TOMATOES

SERVES 2–3

It takes only a few minutes to prepare and make this simple savoury pasta.

4tbsp olive oil
1 small onion, chopped
2 garlic cloves, chopped
6 dried tomato halves, sliced
salt and pepper
7oz (200g) can tuna, drained and flaked
2tsp fresh oregano or parsley
8oz (225g) dried pasta, macaroni or penne

Heat the oil in a saucepan and fry the onion until it softens, then add the garlic. Stir in the tomatoes, salt and pepper and cook for 5 minutes over a low heat. Add the tuna fish and oregano or parsley and heat through for 2 minutes.

Cook the pasta in boiling salted water for the required length of time, then drain and place in a warmed serving dish.

Pour the sauce over the pasta.

Can be served with a sprinkling of grated parmesan cheese on top if desired.

INDIAN SPICED LAMB WITH RAITA

SERVES 2–3

This is a meal which Shula prepared one evening when Mark had invited Usha Gupta, his business partner, to dinner. Raita provides a cool, refreshing accompaniment to the lamb curry.

3tbsp cooking oil
2 medium onions, finely chopped
1lb (450g) fillet of lamb, trimmed and cut into bite-size pieces
1tsp chilli powder
½in (1.25cm) piece fresh root ginger, peeled and chopped
3 cloves garlic, peeled and chopped
1½tsp turmeric
½tsp ground coriander
½tsp cumin seeds
½tsp garam masala
4fl oz (100ml) yogurt
4fl oz (100ml) water
salt

FOR THE RAITA
8fl oz (225ml/½pt) plain yogurt
6oz (175g) cucumber, chopped, or coarsely grated and squeezed dry
1tbsp freshly chopped mint
salt and pepper

Heat the oil in a heavy-based saucepan and fry the onions until soft but not brown. Remove to a plate.

Fry the lamb, stirring and turning until it is browned. Remove to the plate.

Put the chilli powder, ginger, garlic and all the other spices into the pan. Stir in the yogurt and water and bring to simmering point.

Return the lamb and onions to the pan, add salt and simmer the curry slowly for 40–50 minutes.

Serve with raita and rice, with naan bread to soak up the sauce.

To make the raita, mix all the ingredients together and serve in a separate bowl. A pinch of crushed coriander can be added for a spicier taste.

FONDUE BOURGUIGNONNE

Shula has always found fondue entertaining fun and relaxing, with the bonus of little preparation.

Allow 6–8oz (175–225g) steak per person (fillet or rump is ideal), trimmed and cut into bite-size pieces. Lean chicken breast is good too, or a mixture of both.

Accompany the meat with a simple crisp green salad of frisée, served without a dressing as the selection of sauces adds sufficient variety, and hot garlic and herb bread.

SAUCES

Avocado, puréed with lemon juice and mayonnaise.

Aïoli – mayonnaise blended with crushed garlic cloves.

Yogurt, combined with chopped cucumber and mint.

Fromage frais with Roquefort or Danish blue cheese.

GARLIC AND HERB BREAD

If you haven't any fresh herbs the dried ones will suffice – just!

4oz (100g) softened butter
2 cloves garlic, peeled and crushed
2tbsp freshly chopped herbs (parsley, coriander, chives, tarragon) or 2tsp dried herbs
salt and black pepper
1 large or 2 small sticks of French bread

Put the butter in a basin with the garlic, herbs and seasoning, and blend together thoroughly.

Cut vertical slits in the bread at approximately 1in intervals, taking care not to cut right through.

Spread the butter and herb mixture between each slice of bread, reserving a little to spread on the top of the loaf.

Wrap in foil and bake in a fairly hot oven at 375°F/190°C/Gas 5 for about 15 minutes.

Serve the bread hot.

FRUIT BRÛLÉE

SERVES 3–4

A delicious and simple choice for entertaining in the summer when soft fruits are plentiful.

1lb (450g) soft fruits (eg raspberries, mulberries, strawberries, blackcurrants etc)
3oz (75g) caster sugar
6fl oz (175ml) double cream
6fl oz (175ml) whole milk yogurt
6oz (175g) demerara or soft brown sugar

Place the fruit in a saucepan over a moderate heat. Add the caster sugar and heat until the sugar has dissolved. Place in a shallow oven-proof dish and allow to cool.

Whip the cream until thick and then fold in the yogurt. Spread this mixture carefully over the fruit right up to the edges of the dish. Thickly sprinkle the demerara sugar on to the cream.

Preheat the grill to its highest setting and place the dish under for about 3 minutes, until the sugar is bubbling and caramelised.

Chill before serving.

COUNTRY · CUTTINGS

Old Mrs Blossom used to flavour her tea by keeping some dried orange peel in the caddy.

BLUE CHEESE DIP

SERVES 6

Danish blue is quite acceptable in this recipe but I think Roquefort makes it extra special.

4oz (100g) Roquefort or Danish blue cheese
3oz (75g) softened cream cheese
4tbsp corn oil
½tsp salt

Combine all the ingredients in a food processor or blender until smooth. Serve with crudités.

PRAWN DIP WITH CRUDITÉS

SERVES 6–8

So quick and easy to prepare, this dip is a firm favourite with all at Home Farm. If you haven't time to make the mayonnaise buy a good quality creamy one – and add a squeeze of lemon juice.

6oz (175g) prawns, frozen or fresh
6tbsp mayonnaise
3tbsp milk
1½oz (40g) cheddar cheese, cut into cubes
1 small onion, chopped
1tsp Worcester sauce

Combine all the ingredients in a food processor or blender until smooth.

Serve with crudités – raw vegetables suitable for dipping into such sauces. Cut carrot, celery, courgettes, celeriac and sweet peppers into little sticks, and cauliflower into small florets.

MAYONNAISE

(FOR THE PRAWN DIP)

2 medium size egg yolks
½tsp salt
¼tsp white pepper
1tsp Dijon mustard
a few drops of lemon juice
½tsp caster sugar
10fl oz (275ml/½pt) olive oil
2tbsp wine vinegar

In a food processor or blender combine the egg yolks, seasonings, sugar and lemon juice. Blend thoroughly, adding the olive oil in a steady stream. When thoroughly amalgamated, add the vinegar and adjust the seasoning. If you find it is too thick, add a little water.

To make a garlic mayonnaise, add two cloves of garlic with the egg yolks.

Keep mayonnaise in a screw-topped jar in the refrigerator for no longer than 3 days.

COFFEE MORNING

'DON'T KNOCK, JUST ENTER,' we were instructed at No 1 the council houses, opposite the village green. 'Dunroamin', faintly painted over, sneered through satin-finished weather-boarding.

The veneered mahogany door stood proudly ajar. A serviceable square of 'see-thru' plastic protected the apparently pristine state of the 100 per cent acrylic, flecked shagpile in the compact hallway.

'Come on, come in!'

A small, embarrassed group clustered in the lounge, admiring Susan Carter's grinning gallery of family photographs. Filigree-framed Carters and Horrobins were in frightening profusion – with the exception of Clive, conspicuous by his absence – on the lacquered ledge. The three-bar 'electric' gave off a stuffy heat in the small, square room. Sugary icing slowly melted on the biscuits balancing on a 'Present from Great Yarmouth' plate. Colourful bric-à-brac, easily mistaken for the Bring and Buy, was carefully arranged on the lace-matted sideboard.

Sounds of chinking and rattling from the kitchen reached a crescendo when Betty, resplendent in a frilly, flowery pinny, appeared with a laden tray. Susan's friendly stalwarts sank thankfully on to the sofa's edge, stirring and sipping, delighted with the familiar taste of this steaming, straight-from-the-jar-with-a-gold-top coffee.

WHOLEWHEAT CHEESE SCONES

MAKES 12

A good, mature cheddar is a must for these scones. Auntie Christine makes deliciously light scones, sometimes adding some freshly snipped chives, or finely chopped celery to this recipe, which makes about a dozen scones.

4oz (100g) wholewheat flour
4oz (100g) self-raising flour
a pinch salt
1tsp (level) baking powder
2oz (50g) butter or margarine
3–4oz (75–100g) finely grated cheddar cheese
1tsp (level) dry mustard powder
a pinch of cayenne pepper
5fl oz (150ml/¼pt) milk

Sift the flours, salt and baking powder together in a mixing bowl. Rub in the butter until the mixture resembles fine breadcrumbs. Stir in half the cheese, the mustard power and cayenne pepper and mix lightly together with enough milk to make a soft dough.

Turn on to a floured surface and roll out to about ¾in thick. Cut into rounds with a 2½in scone cutter. Brush the tops of the scones with milk and sprinkle with the remainder of the cheese.

Bake on a large, greased baking sheet at 425°F/220°C/Gas 7 for about 10 minutes. Then, allow to cool on a wire rack.

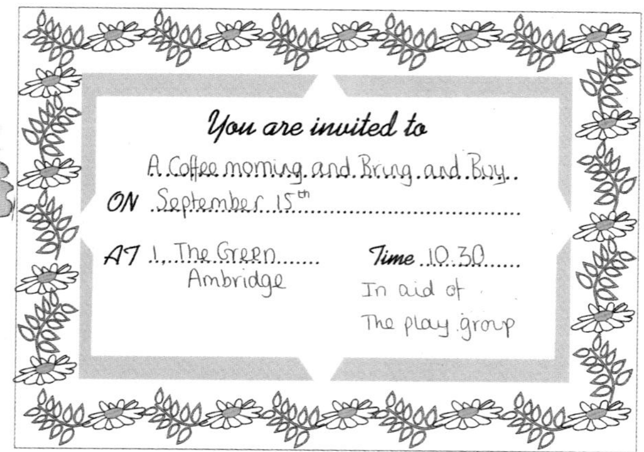

FRUITY FLORENTINES

MAKES ABOUT 20

With these in the oven the kitchen smells deliciously of a French patisserie.

4oz (100g) butter or margarine
4oz (100g) caster sugar
2tbsp clear honey
2tbsp mixed peel, chopped
2tbsp glacé cherries, chopped
1tbsp sultanas
1tbsp blanched almonds, chopped
4oz (100g) plain flour
4oz (100g) plain chocolate

Line baking sheets with non-stick parchment. Melt the butter in a saucepan, stir in the sugar and honey and bring slowly to the boil while stirring. Remove from the heat and add the mixed peel, cherries, sultanas, almonds and flour. Stir thoroughly and allow to cool slightly.

Drop heaped teaspoons of the mixture on to the baking sheets, allowing space to spread, and bake for 10–12 minutes at 350°F/180°C/Gas 4 until golden brown.

Allow to cool for 1–2 minutes before removing with a palette knife. Place on a wire tray to cool further.

Melt the chocolate in a basin over a pan of boiling water, then spoon and spread the chocolate over the smooth surface of each biscuit, making swirled patterns with a fork.

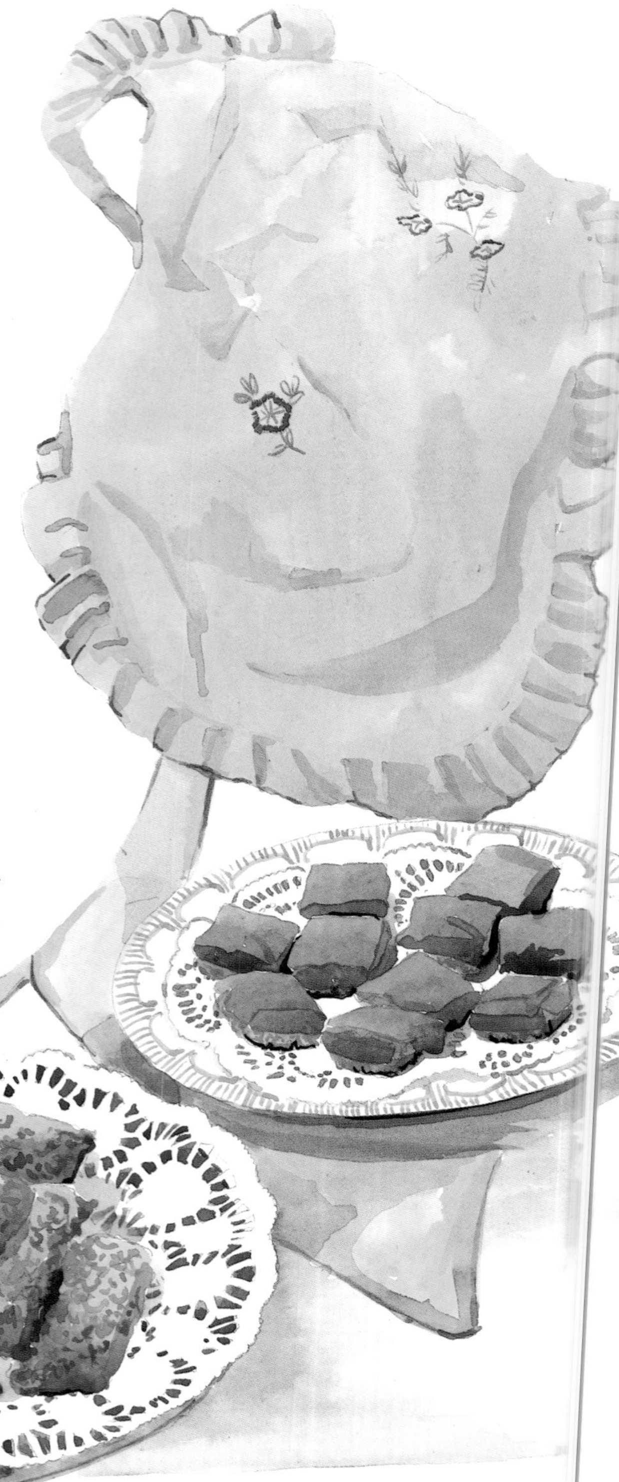

LEMON-ICED SHORTBREAD

MAKES ABOUT 20

Tangy and decidedly moreish, the ground rice gives these biscuits an interesting texture.

4oz (100g) butter
2oz (50g) caster sugar
grated rind of ½ lemon
4oz (100g) plain flour
2oz (50g) ground rice

FOR THE LEMON ICING
1tbsp hot water
1tbsp lemon juice
4oz (100g) icing sugar, sieved

Cream the butter and the sugar together until soft. Beat in the grated lemon rind. Stir in the flour and ground rice and mix to a smooth dough.

Roll the dough out thinly and cut out rounds with a fluted biscuit cutter. Place the rounds on greased baking sheets and prick the surface with a fork. Bake in the oven at 350°F/180°C/Gas 4 for 15 minutes, or until golden.

To make the icing, add the water and lemon juice to the icing sugar and mix until smooth. When the biscuits are cool, spread on the icing.

TOFFEE SQUARES

Strictly not for those on a diet – these are too scrumptious for chocolate-loving sweet-tooths!

FOR THE SHORTBREAD BASE
4oz (100g) butter or margarine
2oz (50g) caster sugar
4oz (100g) self-raising flour
½tsp vanilla essence

Cream the butter and sugar together and add the vanilla essence and flour. Mix to a smooth paste and spread into a Swiss roll tin.

Bake in the oven at 350°F/180°C/Gas 4 for 20 minutes or until golden.

FOR THE TOFFEE TOPPING
4oz (100g) soft brown sugar
4oz (100g) butter or margarine
2tbsp golden syrup
1 small (218g) tin condensed milk
6oz (175g) dark chocolate

Melt the sugar, butter, syrup and condensed milk together in a saucepan over a moderate heat until the mixture is thick enough to leave the side of the pan. Bring to the boil, stirring all the time, and boil for 4 minutes. Pour over the shortbread and leave to cool.

Melt 6oz (175g) chocolate and pour over the toffee. Cut into squares when cold.

COUNTRY · CUTTINGS

Auntie Pru always said never bake more than one kind of cake in the oven at one time.

A simple treat for a sweet tooth – stoned dates stuffed with marzipan.

COCONUT FLAPJACKS

MAKES 12–16 FINGERS

Susan Carter says Emma and Christopher prefer these flapjacks when she spreads some melted chocolate on top.

4oz (100g) margarine
3oz (75g) golden syrup
4oz (100g) demerara sugar
6oz (175g) rolled oats
2oz (50g) desiccated coconut
1tsp almond essence

Melt the margarine, sugar and syrup together in a saucepan. Add the oats, coconut and almond essence and mix thoroughly.

Press the mixture into a shallow greased tin 9 x 6in and bake in a preheated oven at 350°F/180°C/Gas 4 for about 30 minutes until golden.

Cool in the tin for 2–3 minutes before cutting into fingers, then remove when cool.

BRIDGE FARM

NATURALLY FRESH-FACED, and by nature a good farmer's wife, Pat Archer stands, white-coated and efficient, watching the steady stirring of a bowl of Ambridge dairy-fresh yogurt.

The swirling creamy mixture is carefully poured into clean, plastic pots, each ostentatiously bearing the seal of organic approval – the Soil Association symbol. Proudly proclaiming its additive- and preservative-free status, the overdue order is for immediate delivery to our useful local village shop. Pat's natural yogurt is produced daily in Bridge Farm's dairy from fresh milk straight from the udders of cud-chewing cows.

Beyond the dull red-brick farmhouse of tenant farmer Tony Archer lies a pretty patchwork of thistle-free fields. Old-style plots studded with bushes and boxed with high hedges are farmed with old-fashioned implements in a traditional way.

On frozen-fingered February mornings, earthbound leeks, hand-dug, hand-trimmed and hand-rinsed, are neatly hand-packed in wooden boxes. Earthy orange swedes are bagged. Caterpillar-free cabbages are cut and crated. All are stacked and waiting for the all-important co-operative collection.

In early summer, the healthy carrot crops, weeded by willing low-paid hands, are fed on rich slurry; later, sweet-smelling cows are fed on the chopped-off carrot tops. After harvest, with autumn on the way, the free-range chickens scratch and forage in corn-sprinkled stubble fields.

Using no sprays or pesticides, Pat emphatically and wholeheartedly believes, as does her furrow-browed husband Tony, in this wholesome, wholewheat philosophy of farming.

CRUNCHY APPLE SALAD WITH HERB DRESSING

SERVES 4–6

A simple starter that is both satisfying and full of goodness. For hungry farmers, place the salad on crustless wholemeal bread cut with a scone cutter. The salad can also be converted to a light lunchtime snack by the addition of flaked fillets of cold smoked mackerel.

Garnish with lemon wedges and serve on a bed of lettuce.

FOR THE HERB DRESSING
10oz (275g) natural yogurt
3 spring onions, finely chopped
1tbsp snipped chives
1tbsp chopped fresh parsley
1tbsp chopped mint
½tsp curry powder
salt and freshly ground black pepper

4 dessert apples (Cox's Orange Pippins are ideal)
juice of 1 lemon
2oz (50g) chopped walnuts
2oz (50g) sultanas
1tbsp horseradish cream

First, make the dressing by mixing all those ingredients together – thin with a little lemon juice if necessary. (Reserve a few chives for a garnish.)

For the salad, wash, core and chop the apples, but do not peel them. Toss in the lemon juice to prevent discolouration. Mix together with the chopped walnuts and sultanas and then add the horseradish cream.

Pile on to a bed of green salad and pour the herb dressing over. Decorate with a few snipped chives.

COUNTRY·CUTTINGS

Remove a rose thorn or splinter from your finger by applying a paste of bicarbonate of soda.

BRIDGE FARM'S BEST VEGETABLE CASSEROLE

SERVES 4–5

When Pat finds the time, or has help from Sharon or Helen to peel and chop all those home-grown organic vegetables, this is the definitive meal. For the last 15 minutes of cooking, Pat removes the lid and scatters a mixture of wholemeal breadcrumbs, grated cheese and herbs on the top. This forms a delicious crumbly crust.

4oz (100g) lentils
2tbsp vegetable oil
2 onions, peeled and finely chopped
2 cloves garlic, peeled and chopped
2 sticks celery, finely chopped
3 small turnips, chopped into small cubes
4 carrots, diced
4 leeks, cleaned and sliced
2 parsnips, diced
20fl oz (600ml/1pt) vegetable or chicken stock
1tbsp parsley
1tbsp dried mixed herbs
salt and pepper

Soak the lentils in cold water overnight, then drain.

Heat the oil in a frying pan and sauté the onion, garlic and celery until slightly browned. Add the root vegetables and cook for 5 minutes, turning them in the oil. Add the lentils to the frying pan with the stock and stir over a low heat until simmering. Add the herbs and salt, pour into a casserole, cover and cook for 1–1½ hours in a cool oven at 300°F/150°C/Gas 2.

Serve with hot baked potatoes and a green vegetable.

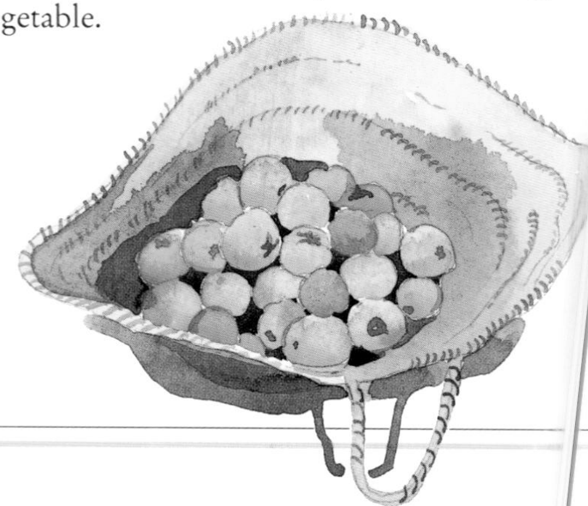

JOHN'S BUBBLE AND SQUEAK

SERVES AT LEAST 2

There is usually a dish of left-over mashed potato in the larder, and some remains of the previous day's cooked greens. As dull as they were then, they always taste much more exciting mixed together and cooked John's way. Tommy insists on lashings of tomato ketchup, and even John admits a generous shake of Worcester sauce makes the finished dish even more scrummy.

8oz (225g) cold cabbage or brussels sprouts
1lb (450g) mashed potato
1tbsp oil
1 small onion
3 rashers green streaky bacon
salt and pepper
3oz (75g) grated cheese

Chop the cabbage and mix with the potato.

Heat the oil in a frying pan, add the chopped onion and the bacon, which has been snipped into thin strips. When the onion is soft, add the potato and cabbage mixture and press down firmly. Season with salt and pepper and fry until the bottom is brown.

Sprinkle the grated cheese on the top and brown under the grill.

RICH BEEF RAGOÛT

SERVES 4

Tony is told emphatically that this is not just 'stew'. As soon as he realises the rich sauce is alcohol-based he's happy. He enjoys a baked potato topped with horseradish cream to accompany this dish.

2lb (1kg) chuck or braising steak
2tbsp vegetable oil
1 large chopped onion
2tbsp plain flour
rind and juice of 1 orange
10fl oz (275ml/ ½pt) pale ale
1tbsp redcurrant jelly
1tbsp tomato purée
salt and pepper
bay leaf

Cut the meat into bite-size pieces and fry in the oil, a few pieces at a time, browning on all sides. Remove from the pan and place in a casserole.

Fry the onion until soft and transparent. Stir in the flour and cook for 1 minute. Add the rind and juice of the orange and the ale, stirring until it comes to the boil. Stir in the redcurrant jelly, tomato purée and seasoning.

Pour over the meat, add the bay leaf and cook at 300°F/150°C/Gas 2 for 2–2½ hours.

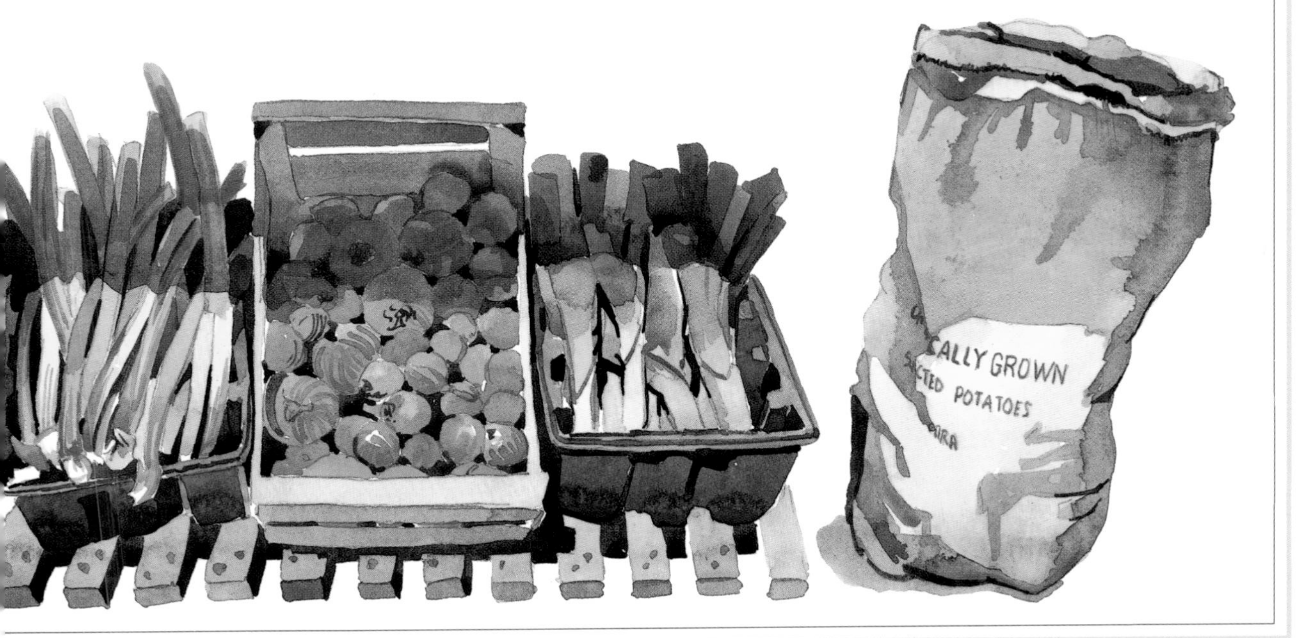

Glazed Parsnips and Carrots

SERVES 6

This mélange of organic root vegetables is ideal with any roast meat, but is particularly good with beef and Yorkshire pudding.

1lb (450g) carrots
1lb (450g) parsnips
pinch of salt
2oz (50g) butter
grated rind and juice of 1 orange
½oz (15g) caster sugar
chopped parsley to garnish

Peel and slice the carrots thinly. Peel and quarter the parsnips, cutting out the woody centres before slicing them thickly. Put the vegetables in a pan, covering with water, add the salt and boil until barely tender.

Drain, then add the butter, orange rind and juice and sugar to the vegetables in the pan. Cook steadily at first, then more vigorously, shaking the pan. The juice will reduce and form a glaze. Serve sprinkled with chopped parsley.

Saturday Sausage Bake

SERVES 4

A whole meal in one pot – that has to be helpful to a busy farmer's wife. Pat often serves this with hot wholemeal rolls as an accompaniment.

1tbsp oil
1lb (450g) thick pork sausages
6 rashers streaky bacon, cut into strips
2 leeks, sliced
2 onions, chopped
1tbsp flour
2 potatoes, thinly sliced
8oz (225g) can tomatoes
2tbsp tomato purée
10fl oz (275ml/ ½pt) stock or cider
salt and pepper

Heat the oil in a flameproof casserole and fry the sausages. When browned, remove from the casserole, cut them through lengthways and reserve. Add the bacon, leeks and onion and fry until the onion is soft. Add the flour and cook for a further 2–3 minutes.

Return the sausages to the casserole with the potatoes, tomatoes and tomato purée. Add the stock or cider and season.

Cover and bake in the oven at 375°F/190°C/Gas 5 for an hour or until the potatoes are soft.

Pat suggests adding chopped walnuts or hazelnuts to wholemeal scones – makes an autumnal tea-time treat.

Courgette Cheese Tart

SERVES 4–6

This is a versatile tart which can be served cold with salad and parsleyed new potatoes, or hot straight from the oven with its filling still puffy and light. I would be tempted to use some crushed garlic in with the courgettes to add a little extra oomph.

For the Cheese Pastry

6oz (175g) plain flour
½tsp salt
pinch cayenne pepper
pinch dry mustard
2oz (50g) butter or margarine
2oz (50g) finely grated cheddar cheese
2tbsp cold water

For the Filling

12oz (350g) courgettes
1oz (25g) butter
1 medium chopped onion
¼tsp grated nutmeg
5fl oz (150ml/ ¼pt) natural yogurt or single cream
2 large size eggs or 3 smaller ones
2tbsp grated parmesan cheese
salt and pepper

Sift the flour, salt, pepper and mustard into a bowl. Rub in the butter until the mixture resembles fine breadcrumbs. Mix in the cheese and sprinkle on the cold water, then knead lightly to form a smooth dough, adding more water if necessary.

Roll out the pastry to line an 8in flan tin. Prick the base and bake blind at an oven temperature of 375°F/190°C/Gas 5 for 15–20 minutes, or until the pastry is just set.

To make the filling, wash the courgettes, cut off the stalks, but do not peel, and dice.

Melt the butter, add the onion, courgettes and nutmeg and cook over a low heat until the courgettes are just tender. Leave to cool.

Beat the eggs, yogurt, parmesan and seasoning together. Combine with the courgettes and pour into the pastry case. Bake for 30–40 minutes at 350°F/180°C/Gas 4.

CARROT AND ORANGE SOUP

The joy of both the following soups is that they can be served either hot with crusty rolls or croutons in the winter, or cold with swirls of cream or yogurt and sprinkled with freshly snipped herbs on a balmy summer evening.

SERVES 6

1lb (450g) carrots
1 medium onion
2oz (50g) butter or 2tbsp vegetable oil
2tsp sugar
1tsp mace
salt and pepper
40fl oz (1.2L/2pt) chicken stock (or use a stock cube)
grated rind and juice of 1 large orange
5fl oz (150ml/ ¼pt) natural yogurt

Peel and chop the carrots and onion. Heat the butter in a large saucepan, add the carrot and onion and cook over a low heat for 10 minutes.

Add the sugar, mace and seasoning and stir while adding the stock. Bring to the boil, then cover and simmer until tender.

Allow to cool a little, and then either put through a sieve or blend in a food processor until smooth. Stir in the orange rind and juice.

Pour the soup into individual bowls adding a swirl of yogurt to serve.

LEEK AND POTATO SOUP

SERVES 6

2oz (50g) butter
2 onions, chopped
1lb (450g) leeks
1lb (450g) potatoes, diced
1tsp Dijon mustard
30fl oz (900ml/1½pt) chicken stock (or use a stock cube)
salt and pepper
5fl oz (150ml/ ¼pt) natural yogurt or single cream
chopped chives

Melt the butter in a large saucepan. Add the onions, roughly chopped leeks and potatoes. Toss in the butter and stir, cooking for 5 minutes. Add the mustard, stock and seasoning. Bring to the boil, then cover and simmer for 30 minutes.

Allow to cool slightly, strain off the liquid and either sieve the vegetables or put through a blender. Gradually mix the liquid into the purée.

When ready to serve add the cream or yogurt and garnish with chopped chives.

COUNTRY · CUTTINGS

Pat makes special pastry for fruit pies using half margarine and half cream cheese. Mix with lemon juice and add a little water to make a soft dough with plain flour.

Uncle Walter's winter warming orange wine – Boil the rind of 8 large oranges and 4 lemons in 4.5L (8pt) of water. Add the juice of the fruit and 4lb (1.8kg) sugar and stir until dissolved. Sieve and bottle, adding a few large raisins, some bruised ginger root and a clove to each bottle. Leave at room temperature to ferment. Cork.

Blackberry Butterscotch Cream

SERVES 4–6

Based on a typical Danish dessert, Thorkil suggested this superb recipe to Pat.

2 large cooking apples
1lb (450g) freshly picked blackberries
3tbsp clear honey
½tsp cinnamon or ½ cinnamon stick
5fl oz (150ml/ ¼pt) double cream
5fl oz (150ml/ ¼pt) yogurt

FOR THE TOPPING
3oz (75g) unsalted butter
4oz (100g) coarse white breadcrumbs
1oz (25g) caster sugar

Peel and slice the apples and put with the rinsed blackberries in a saucepan. Add the honey and cinnamon and simmer over a low heat until the fruit is soft.

Remove the cinnamon stick, allow the fruit to cool a little and put into a glass bowl.

Whip the cream, adding the yogurt spoonful by spoonful until thick. Keep to one side until the topping is made.

For the topping, melt the butter in a clean frying pan and add the breadcrumbs and sugar. Gently brown the breadcrumbs, stirring to prevent them from burning. When golden brown, spread out on to a large plate to cool.

Sprinkle some of these crunchy crumbs on to the fruit. Put the cream/yogurt mixture on top and the remaining crumbs as a final layer.

COUNTRY · CUTTINGS

Bert Fry's liquid compost – Soak nettles or comfrey leaves in a large bucket of rain water. (Watch out for the appalling smell!)

'Tea made with an infusion of wild thyme works wonders for hangovers,' Tony says.

Eva's Apfelkuchen

Many years ago this recipe was given to Pat by Eva Lenz, the au pair at Home Farm. It has withstood the test of time and is still a favourite. Pat serves it with dollops of thick yogurt.

4oz (100g) butter
4oz (100g) caster sugar
8oz (225g) self-raising flour
1 medium size egg
1lb (450g) cooking apples
1tbsp brown sugar
1oz (25g) sultanas
1tsp cinnamon
a little icing sugar

Grease and line a loose-bottomed 8in cake tin. Melt the butter in a saucepan over a low heat and add the sugar. Sift the flour into a bowl and combine with the beaten egg. Then stir in the butter and sugar mixture.

Peel, core and slice the apples. Put in a bowl and mix with the brown sugar, sultanas and cinnamon. Spread half the cake mixture in the bottom of the tin, arranging the spiced sugar and apple on top. Cover with the remaining cake mixture. (This is rather difficult and it doesn't matter if you leave gaps.)

Place the cake tin in a preheated oven at 350°F/180°C/Gas 4 and bake for about an hour or until golden.

Cool in the tin and either dust with icing sugar or drizzle over a thin icing glaze.

BATTERED PLUM BAKE

SERVES 4–6

Based on a French recipe which uses black cherries, this excellent and easy pudding can equally well be made with fresh plums. Young, tender sticks of rhubarb sprinkled with ground ginger are delicious too.

1lb (450g) small sweet plums
6oz (175g) plain flour
pinch of salt
3 medium size eggs
3oz (75g) caster sugar
10fl oz (275ml/½pt) milk
a few drops almond essence
1tsp ground cinnamon
a little icing sugar

Cut the washed plums into halves or quarters depending on their size and lay them skin side up on a greased baking dish.

Sieve the flour and salt into a bowl. Add the beaten eggs and sugar. Gradually stir in the milk and almond essence and beat until smooth. Pour the mixture over the plums and sprinkle with ground cinnamon.

Bake for 35–40 minutes at 350°F/180°C/Gas 4. Dust with icing sugar before serving.

FROZEN FRUIT YOGURT

SERVES 6–8

Pat is truly expert at concocting delectable recipes for yogurt ice-cream. Here is one that is a great favourite with Alice – probably because it's a lovely pink!

8oz (225g) raspberries
8oz (225g) strawberries
8oz (225g) caster sugar
1tbsp lemon juice
20fl oz (600ml/1pt) natural whole milk yogurt
2 medium size egg whites

Wash the fruit and purée it by rubbing through a sieve. Sweeten it with the sugar, and add the lemon juice and yogurt, stirring thoroughly.

Beat the egg whites until stiff and fold these into the purée. Pour into a plastic container and freeze until firm but not fully frozen.

Remove from the freezer and beat with an electric mixer, or by hand with a rotary whisk, to break down the ice crystals. Return to the freezer. Repeat this partial freezing and beating process once more.

Allow at least 10 minutes out of the freezer before serving.

Ambridge Flower And Produce Show

There was a chill in the morning air, the grass was damp and dewlogged, and stubble in the fields was dappled ochre in the autumn light. This was the time of year when a dormouse would stretch, twitch its whiskers, then curl up and sleep on – but not Bert Fry.

Shirt sleeves purposefully rolled up, gum-booted and grim-faced, he pushed his heavy squeaking barrow in the direction of the village hall, its sack-covered contents a bulky secret. Some paces behind, a breathless, flower-frocked Freda hurried, she too with a mysterious load in a wicker basket covered in white linen.

Today was the day, the one they'd been waiting for, the one they'd been working for. For weeks now Bert had been spraying, watering and feeding, and fighting a war against grubs and slugs. Meanwhile Freda had picked and pickled, simmered and bottled.

Inside the hall there was an air of teasing smells and tempting success and Ambridge's cottagers were milling and babbling with excitement. Standing neatly on trestle tables, pinned with paper cloths, were bottles and jars in rank and file, obeying judges' orders. All were clearly labelled – sherbert-bright lemon curd, tawny, chunky marmalade, rose-red jam. Golden Madeira cakes sat trapped under clingy-clear food-wrap awaiting the judges' knife-sharp incision, their crumby-lipped decision.

Vivid spears of gladioli towered above vulgar pompom dahlias and jars of unassuming Michaelmas daisies. In dumpy pottery pots and earthenware mugs were the children's

treasures – unpretentious posies, wind-blown flowers from wood and hedgerow, all instantly appealing in their innocent simplicity.

In a place of honour, proudly displayed on the platform, stood the greatly coveted 'Lawson Hope Challenge Cup', awarded to the best entry in the show.

A kaleidoscope of colour was reflected in its polished silver sheen – the greyish-green of crinkly crisp cabbages, the saffron orange of scrubbed carrots, the billiard-ball red of tomatoes – but pompously upstaging all else was Bert Fry's supremely placed monstrous yellow pumpkin.

MADEIRA CAKE

All candidates entering the Madeira cake class should follow this recipe.

6oz (175g) butter, softened
6oz (175g) caster sugar
3 medium size eggs, beaten
grated rind of 1 lemon
8oz (225g) plain flour
2tsp (level) baking powder
milk and water to mix
2 strips citron peel

Cream the butter and sugar together until pale and fluffy. Add the eggs and lemon rind and beat again. Stir in the sifted flour and baking powder alternately with the milk and water. Mix thoroughly.

Put into a greased and lined 7in round cake tin and bake in the oven at 350°F/180°C/Gas 4. After ½ hour place the citron peel on the mixture and continue to bake for a further 1–1½ hours until cooked. (Test with a skewer, which should come away clean.)

Turn the cake out and allow to cool on a wire rack.

STORAGE TIPS

Most jams, if there is a high enough sugar content and they are stored in a cool, dark, dry and well-ventilated place, should keep for up to a year. After that time the flavour could deteriorate.

Chutneys and pickles should be stored in jars with vinegar-proof or plastic-lined lids. Kept in similar conditions to jams they should mature after two months.

THE PARGETTERS' PINEAPPLE AND LIME MARMALADE

It's utterly impossible to imagine Julia standing and stirring a bubbling cauldron of boiling marmalade; however, this is one of Nigel's favourites.

1½lb (675g) limes (approximately 9 limes)
1 large pineapple
80fl oz (2.3L/4pt) water
6lb (2.75kg) granulated or preserving sugar (approximately – reduce to 4½lb/2kg for a sharper flavour)

Wash the limes and squeeze and reserve the juice. Remove the flesh from the peel – this is easiest with the end of a teaspoon, or with your thumb – and tie in a muslin bag. Cut the peel into fine shreds.

Peel the pineapple, removing the woody core and any 'eyes'. Chop the flesh, reserving the juice.

Place all the fruit in a large bowl, add sufficient water to the fruit juices to make 2.3L (4pt), pour over and soak overnight.

Transfer to a preserving pan and simmer for about an hour, until the lime peel is tender and the liquid is reduced by half. Remove the muslin bag, add the warmed sugar and stir over a low heat until dissolved. Then boil rapidly until the marmalade sets on a cold plate.

Pour into warm, clean glass jars, cover and label.

MARTHA'S MARROW, LEMON AND GINGER JAM

This syrupy, lumpy jam can be used in tarts and pastry dumplings.

3lb (1.5kg) marrow
3lb (1.5kg) granulated or preserving sugar
juice and grated rind of 3 lemons
1tsp ground ginger
4oz (100g) crystallised ginger, chopped

Peel, seed and chop the marrow into 1in/2cm dice. Weigh, and place in a bowl. Measure the same weight of sugar, and add two-thirds to the marrow. Leave overnight. Transfer to a preserving pan, add the lemon rind and juice, bring to the boil and cook for 30 minutes.

Add the remaining sugar and ginger and boil gently until setting point is reached and the marrow is transparent. Pot, seal and label.

COUNTRY · CUTTINGS

To delicately flavour apple purée or jelly, add a scented pelargonium leaf when boiling the apples.

AUTUMN JAM

A great recipe for using up those windfalls. Delicious with a crust of bread and cheese, or to fill pies and pastry dumplings. Freda Fry says she likes to put a cinnamon stick in to flavour the apples as they're softening.

4lb (2kg) cooking apples, peeled and chopped
grated rind and juice of 1 large lemon
4oz (100g) chopped mixed peel
20fl oz (600ml/1pt) cold water
cinnamon stick (optional)
4lb (2kg) granulated or preserving sugar

Put the apples in a pan with the water, lemon juice, rind and mixed peel and bring slowly to the boil. Reduce the heat, cover and simmer gently until the apples are soft. Remove cinnamon stick

Stir in the warmed sugar and when this has completely dissolved bring to a rolling boil. Boil rapidly until the jam coats the back of the wooden spoon with which it is stirred.

Put into warm jars, label and cover with waxed paper discs. When cold, cover with dampened rounds of cellophane and secure with a rubber band. Eat within 4–6 weeks.

AUNTIE PRU'S SWEET PICKLED CINNAMON PEARS

'Always use an enamel saucepan and wooden spoon when you're making chutneys and pickles,' Auntie Pru used to tell me. And she knew: her pickles were the finest in South Borsetshire. This one is excellent with slices of cold ham or turkey.

3lb (1.5kg) granulated sugar
20fl oz (600ml/1pt) malt vinegar
4lb (2kg) pears (Conference are ideal)
1tbsp whole cloves
1tbsp allspice berries
1 small piece root ginger
1 cinnamon stick
rind of ½ lemon, peeled and cut into strips

Put the sugar and vinegar into a preserving pan and heat gently. Peel and core the pears and cut into quarters. Add the pears and all the spices and simmer until the pears are tender.

Remove the pears to warm, clean jars, boil the syrup for a further 15 minutes and then pour over the pears in the jars, including the spices.

Cover the pots, seal and label.

COUNTRY · CUTTINGS

Auntie Pru's recipe for pickling vinegar – Add a stick of cinnamon, a few red chillies, whole cloves, black peppercorns, mace and allspice berries to the vinegar while heating. Bring to the boil, then cool, strain and bottle.

To remove the scum from the surface of freshly boiled jam or marmalade either drop in a knob of butter or blot with sheets of kitchen roll.

CLARRIE'S CRUNCHY CHUTNEY

Out of the cold easterly wind into the warmth of Clarrie's kitchen, with a jug of cider at his elbow, Joe revels in a stockman's snack – a hunk of Lizzie Larkin's Loaf (see p116), a chunk of good strong cheddar and a spoonful of his favourite chutney. The delight of this is it needs no cooking, so there's no need to pervade the house with the nose-tingling smells of boiling vinegar.

1lb (450g) dates
1lb (450g) sultanas
1lb (450g) apples, cored, unpeeled and chopped
1lb (450g) onions
1lb (450g) dark brown moist sugar
20fl oz (600ml/1pt) malt vinegar
1tsp salt
½tsp ginger
1tsp dry mustard

Mince the dates and sultanas, cored apples and peeled onions. Put in a large bowl with the sugar, vinegar and spices and stir thoroughly. Leave for 24 hours stirring occasionally.

Pot in clean jars, label and seal.

THREE FRUIT HONEY MARMALADE

This is Jill Archer's recipe using some of her own honey. This can also be made using muscovado sugar for a darker marmalade, although you will achieve a softer set.

3 grapefruits
3 sweet oranges
3 lemons
3lb (1.5kg) clear honey
80fl oz (2.3L/4pt) water

Wash and dry the fruit. Squeeze the juice, remove the flesh and pips and tie them in a muslin bag. Place the juice and bag in a preserving pan, and add the finely sliced peel. Add the water, boil and simmer for about 2 hours.

Remove the muslin bag. Stir in the honey until it has dissolved and then boil rapidly until set. Pull the preserving pan to one side off the heat when testing for setting point – this marmalade can overcook very easily.

Skim, leave to cool for 30–45 minutes, then pour into warmed jars and seal and label.

CAROL TREGORRAN'S BRANDIED APRICOT AND ALMOND CONSERVE

This can be used as an instant dessert with fromage frais and a finger of shortbread. Conserves have a 'softer' set than jams.

2lb (1kg) dried apricots
80fl oz (2.3L/4pt) water
4 lemons
4lb (2kg) preserving sugar
3½oz (90g) flaked almonds
5fl oz (150ml/ ¼pt) brandy

Soak the dried apricots in water overnight. Strain the fruit and reserve the liquid. Roughly chop the fruit.

Pour this liquid into a preserving pan with the grated rind of the four lemons and the sugar. Simmer gently until the sugar has dissolved, then boil until the syrup has thickened and reduced by about one-third.

Cut away all the pith from the lemons with a sharp knife and then slice them thinly, and put into the syrup with the apricots. Return to the boil, then boil until the apricots are tender – then stir in the flaked almonds and brandy.

Stand for 1 hour, then pour into warm clean jars. Seal and label.

As conserves do not keep as well as jams it is wise to check them from time to time. Once opened, keep in a refrigerator.

MARTHA WOODFORD'S ROWAN JELLY

The small red-orange berries of the mountain ash make a tart, clear jelly. Martha gave me this recipe to try and so I baked some small vol-au-vent cases (ready frozen from the deep-freeze in the village shop) and spooned in some rowan jelly. So simple and delicious with roast lamb or venison.

3lb (1.5kg) rowan berries
3lb (1.5kg) cooking apples
preserving sugar (see below for amount)

Pick over the berries and roughly chop the unpeeled apples. Put them all in a preserving pan, cover with water and bring to the boil. Simmer until the fruit is pulpy.

Turn out into a jelly bag and let it drip, without squeezing, overnight.

Measure the juice and return to the pan. Add the preserving sugar (1lb/450g sugar for each 20fl oz/600ml/1pt juice), and stir on a low heat until dissolved. Then raise the heat and boil until setting point is reached.

Skim off any scum and pour into jars. Cover and label.

Granny Perkins' Crab Apple and Sage Jelly

Using crab apples alone makes the jelly somewhat tart and bitter – maybe pink John Downies with a Borset Pearmain would be a happier compromise, or try replacing some of the water with cider.

3lb (1.5kg) crab apples
60fl oz (1.7L/3pt) water
granulated sugar (see below for amount)
juice of 1 lemon
5tbsp chopped fresh sage

Wash and halve the unpeeled apples. Place in a large pan with the water and bring to the boil. Reduce the heat and simmer until the apples are soft. Ladle the fruit and juice into a jelly bag. Leave to drip but do not squeeze.

Measure the juice and add 1lb (450g) of granulated sugar for every 20fl oz (600ml/1pt) of juice obtained. Place in a preserving pan. Add the lemon juice and most of the chopped sage, and stir over a gentle heat until the sugar has dissolved. Then boil briskly until setting point is reached. Add a small amount of freshly chopped sage.

Pour into clean, warm jars; seal and label when cold. Jelly is best put in small jars to retain its quality when opened.

Note To test for setting: place a small amount of jelly on the edge of a cold plate, and leave to cool. Push a finger carefully through it, and if the surface wrinkles setting point has been reached.

Christine Barford's Spiced Orange Slices

Delicately flavoured, these improve with age and are delicious with cold roast chicken or pork. They make excellent Christmas presents, especially in jolly gingham-topped jars.

6 medium, thin-skinned oranges (unwaxed if possible)
10fl oz (275ml/ ½pt) malt vinegar
1lb (450g) granulated sugar
1 cinnamon stick
½tsp cloves
½tsp whole allspice
½tsp black peppercorns
½tsp coriander seeds

Cover the whole oranges with water and bring to the boil in a large saucepan. Simmer for about an hour until tender. Drain and dry the fruit.

Heat the vinegar, sugar and spices and bring to the boil, stirring until the sugar has dissolved.

Slice the oranges, discard the pips and place in the strained vinegar. Return to the boil and simmer gently for 30 minutes or until glazed.

Transfer the orange slices into warmed jars and boil the remaining syrup until reduced by half. Then pour the syrup over the fruit. Cover when cold.

COUNTRY · CUTTINGS

Freda simmered Bert Fry's pumpkin with a finely chopped onion, adding orange juice to make a delicately flavoured soup.

BETTY'S GOOSEBERRY, ORANGE AND MUSTARD RELISH

Brenda helps Betty top and tail the hairy gooseberries, with the occasional 'it's boring'. But the spicy relish on barbecued burgers makes up for all the moans and groans.

10fl oz (275ml/ ½pt) vinegar
1lb (450g) granulated sugar
grated rind and juice of 3 oranges
1tsp (heaped) ground cloves
1oz (25g) mustard seed
1lb (450g) onions, chopped
2lb (1kg) gooseberries, topped and tailed

Put the vinegar, sugar, orange rind and juice, ground cloves and mustard seed into a large saucepan and slowly bring to the boil.

Add the onions and gooseberries and simmer until the mixture is soft and of a jam-like consistency. Put into warmed jars, cover and label when cold.

HOME-MADE HORSERADISH CREAM

Monday wouldn't be Monday without a good slice of cold sirloin, pink in the middle and spread with horseradish cream. 'Nobody cooked beef like my Pru,' Uncle Tom reminded me.

1lb (450g) horseradish
10fl oz (275ml/ ½pt) vinegar

Clean and scrub the horseradish roots thoroughly. Grate, either in a food processor or with a hand grater. (The horseradish will make your eyes smart and your fingers sore – so this is a labour of love.)

Pack the grated horseradish into jars and cover with white wine vinegar.

To make the cream, mix some of the preserved horseradish with dried mustard powder, soured or double cream and a little sugar. It keeps up to 2 weeks in a covered jar in the refrigerator.

COUNTRY · CUTTINGS

Auntie Pru swore by the herb wormwood. Freshly picked sprigs should be placed in drawers with your woollies, and under the edge of rugs to deter moths.

MRS BLOSSOM'S BLACKBERRY VINEGAR

'A soothing syrup for troublesome coughs' it said on the label. The crumpled recipe came to light at the back of a kitchen drawer at Brookfield.

4lb (2kg) blackberries
40fl oz (1.2L/2pt) malt vinegar
4lb (2kg) brown sugar

Put the cleaned fruit and vinegar into a basin. Stir every other day for a week. Strain through muslin then boil the liquid with the sugar.

Bottle and label when cool.

SHROVE TUESDAY

ORDERS ISSUED BY MARJORIE ANTROBUS. Orders to be obeyed. Number 4 platoon leaves Manorfield Close at 10.45 precisely. 'Company march.' Dressed not in regulation pinafore-style battledress, nor carrying steel frying pans, but clad wisely in well-worn overcoats, pac-a-macs and plastic hoods. Bowed backs battle against the wind. Flailing umbrellas fight the driving rain. 'February fill-dyke – what did I tell yer? You mark my words, they'll call it off.' Uncle Tom's voice full of doom and gloom.

The glistening wheels of Robin Stokes's lengthy Volvo swoosh past the Manorfield manoeuvres. 'A short service of confession . . .' *(short it would have to be)* 'that we *(hastily)* lamenting our sins and *(briefly)* acknowledging our wretchedness' *can release cassock-clad Robin to attend to the pressing problems of Phil Archer's pigs at Brookfield Farm.*

'Company advance.' Leave behind the pounding feet of pancake-tossing Penny Hassett housewives. Swing the snug doors shut against the elements. Shake off the beaded droplets, stamp the feet and sink on to cushioned settles in the comfort of The Griffin's Ploughman's Bar. 'COMPANY, thankfully, HALT.'

OVER SIXTIES OUTING

PENNY HASSETT PANCAKE RACE
February 14th.

ASSEMBLE	Bus shelter on Village Green	10.50 a.m.
DEPART		11.00 a.m.
SERVICE		11.30 a.m.
RACE		12.15 p.m.
LUNCH	(Griffin's Head)	01.00 p.m.

WEAR SENSIBLE CLOTHES

! Those late left behind!

PANCAKES

MAKES 8

This is Jill Archer's traditional pancake recipe. Choose a small omelette or frying pan with a heavy base – and make sure the oil is really hot. The edges of the pancake should be brown and crispy.

4oz (100g) plain flour
pinch salt
1 egg and 1 egg yolk
10fl oz (275ml/ ½pt) milk
1tbsp cooking oil or melted butter

Sift the flour and salt into a mixing bowl. Make a well in the centre and drop in the egg and the extra yolk. Gradually beat or whisk in the milk until the batter is smooth and not lumpy. Leave the batter to rest for 30 minutes, then add the oil and give another whisk. (It should have the consistency of cream.)

Heat the pan until it is really hot, swirl some oil around to coat the base, pouring off any excess.

Add about 2tbsp of batter to the pan and swirl it around evenly. Cook for about a minute until the underside is golden, then turn it or toss it and brown the other side.

The pancakes can either be folded in half and half again, or stacked one on top of the other, and kept warm in a buttered ovenproof dish, covered in foil, in a low oven.

Traditional pancakes are served drenched in lemon juice and sprinkled with sugar.

CAMERON FRASER'S HIGHLAND PANCAKES

In one of his more generous moments Cameron happened to let slip his secret Scottish pancake recipe to Susan Carter, in the estate office one Shrove Tuesday.

4oz (100g) unsalted butter
4oz (100g) caster sugar
½tsp ground ginger
5fl oz (150ml/ ¼pt) freshly squeezed orange juice
grated zest of 1 orange
grated zest of 1 lemon
4tbsp Scotch whisky

Make the pancakes as described before, then soak them in this whisky sauce.

For the whisky sauce, melt the butter, stir in the sugar and ginger, and simmer until the sugar is well dissolved.

Add the juice and grated rind of the oranges and lemons and simmer for 3 minutes, finally adding the whisky.

Pour the sauce over the pancakes.

PARGETTER PANCAKES

After Nigel has learnt the art of making pancakes from Jill Archer – and tossing them too – he races into Borchester, raids the shelves of Underwood's Delicatessen department and treats Elizabeth to an impromptu upmarket lunch.

Make these pancakes with buckwheat flour if possible, to make them closer to Russian blinis.

4fl oz (100ml) thick sour cream (or double cream with added lemon juice)
4oz (100g) smoked saln d
1 small jar lumpfis.

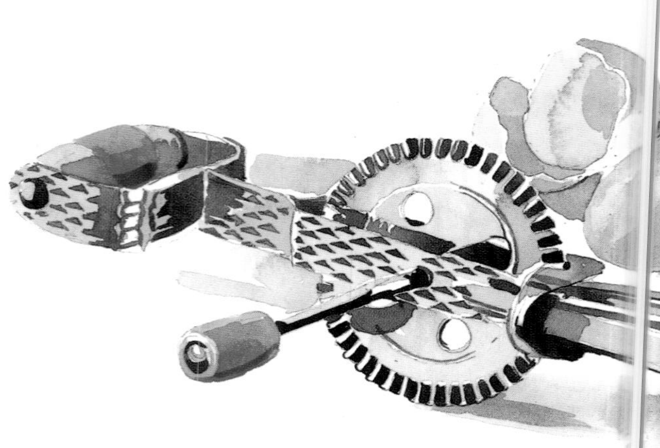

Make the pancakes as before, then while hot, spread them with soured cream, laying on slices of smoked salmon.

Roll the pancakes up, topping each with a dollop of cream and a scattering of 'caviar'.

JEAN PAUL'S CRÊPES AUX POMMES

I prefer Cox's Orange Pippins in this recipe. Bramleys are too soft and French Golden Delicious are dull and tasteless in England, although Jean Paul might not agree.

4 large dessert apples
2oz (50g) butter
4oz (100g) soft brown sugar
juice and grated rind of 1 orange

Peel, core and slice the apples.

Melt the butter in a heavy saucepan and add the apples, sugar, orange juice and rind and cook until the apples are soft.

Make pancakes as described before. Lay the pancakes in a dish one above the other, sandwiching with the apple mixture.

Cover with foil and reheat in a moderate oven 350°F/180°C/Gas 4 for 10 minutes.

Cut into wedges and serve with cream.

CREAMY PRAWN PANCAKES

Why have savoury crêpes or pancakes gone out of fashion? They can be made one day, stuffed and reheated the next. They also adapt well to leftovers. Brian said they were his staple diet when he lived in Paris as a gauche young man. He used to thin down the batter with beer to make the crêpes lighter.

2oz (50g) butter
1 medium onion, chopped
6oz (175g) button mushrooms, sliced
1tsp lemon juice
salt and freshly ground black pepper
a pinch of mace
1oz (25g) plain flour
5–10fl oz (150–275ml / 1/4–1/2pt) milk
8oz (225g) peeled prawns, frozen or fresh
5fl oz (150ml/ 1/4pt) double cream
4tbsp grated cheddar cheese or mozzarella

Make 8 small pancakes as described before and keep warm.

Melt 1oz (25g) butter in a pan and fry the onion until soft and transparent.

In another pan melt the remaining butter and add the mushrooms, lemon juice, salt, pepper and mace.

Stir the flour into the onion when soft, slowly adding the milk and bringing to the boil and stirring until thickened. Add the contents of the mushroom pan, plus the prawns and cream. Reheat, add more milk and season if necessary.

Place some of the mixture on each of the pancakes. Roll them up and place in an ovenproof dish. Sprinkle with the grated cheese and brown under the grill.

COUNTRY · CUTTINGS

Martha's marmalade ideas – Add a cinnamon stick and 1tbsp of black treacle to each pound of fruit to make a dark, rich marmalade.

AMBRIDGE HALL

THE JOURNEY FROM SUNNINGDALE took rather longer than Robert's computerised calculations had predicted, what with lumbering lorries on the A1999 Droitwich to Borchester by-pass and slow-moving tractors on the B3980 Ambridge to Little Croxley by-road. The Snells' four-seater sped past the village green, narrowly missing some Muscovies and Granny Perkins, her bag stuffed with dusters on her way to polish the parish church brasses.

On Lynda's lap lay a smart brochure announcing the sale of 'An interesting Victorian country house, circa 1860. Substantially constructed of yellow brick [at last mellowing] under a hipped, tiled roof, offering well proportioned accommodation: 3 receps., study, large kitchen, utility, larder, usual offices, 6 beds, 2 baths. Useful range of outbuildings [if you can find a range of uses], secluded sheltered gardens and grounds. Fenced [if somewhat haphazardly] paddock. Delightful river frontage. In all about 2.13 acres. Offers invited for the freehold. Viewing strictly by appointment with sole agents Ling and Adair ARICS, London, W1'.

Said agent's assistant waited beneath the 'demi-lune fanlight', impatiently tapping her well-heeled Gucci shoe on the 'tessellated-tiled floor' of the vestibule. Behind her the faded door stood open, liberating the old mustiness which lurked inside the 'large entrance hall with easy-rising main staircase leading to a wide mezzanine landing, offering fine open views of garden and farmland . . .' 'This property would benefit from some modernisation.' Just one of an estate agent's overused understatements.

It was here in Ambridge Hall that loquacious Aunt Laura lived in almost attractive confusion with her erstwhile companion, Freddy Danby. She left behind her a shabby, run-down house, with garden and livestock running wild – not to mention an unsigned will and a homeless Colonel Danby.

Perhaps it was 'the principal reception rooms, spaciously well-proportioned with good ceiling heights' that wooed lofty Lynda and her commuter, nay computer-belted husband from stockbroker Sunningdale. Or maybe her green appetite was whetted by the bee-humming fruit trees, the mossy lawns or the privacy of the wild flower woodland.

St Stephen's clock struck two. Ms Ling and Adair glanced at her watch as the Snells swooped to a stop on the sparsely gravelled carriage sweep. Our prospective purchaser put her new green-booted foot forward and held out her green-fingered hand. The shuttered windows winked in the sudden sunlight and the green roof gleamed at the thought of this nouveau environmentally riche and friendly future.

PIMM'S

Robert and Lynda's secret recipe for a cooling, welcoming glass of Pimm's is to pour a jigger of Pimm's into a tall glass, then add a splash of gin and fill to the brim with Elderflower Pétillant – home-made of course! Add ice cubes, each one frozen with a tiny flower inside it – bright blue borage, violets or pink rose petals. 'No need to float all that cucumber and mint rubbish on it then,' chuckled Robert.

PSYCHEDELIC SPRING SALAD

Using a colourful variety of edible flowers, as well as tender young leaves of dandelions, violets, sorrel and borage, Lynda creates a veritable kaleidoscope of a salad. On a large plate she arranges the fresh green leaves mingled with apple mint, fronds of fennel, mauve chive flowers, sprigs of curly parsley and marigold petals. Later in the year she decorates it with brilliant nasturtium flowers. A mild French dressing made from lemon juice, lime blossom honey and extra virgin olive oil is served separately.

GREEN SPINACH PIE WITH THREE CHEESES

SERVES 4–6

A hugely popular supper dish with Lynda's friends from the Borsetshire Environment Trust – perfectly green in every way! She serves it warm or cold with a colourful salad.

1 medium onion, finely chopped
2 cloves garlic, crushed
8oz (225g) white of leek, thinly sliced
2tbsp olive oil
1lb (450g) young spinach leaves
1oz (25g) fresh wholemeal breadcrumbs
2 medium size eggs
6oz (175g) Ricotta or curd cheese
6oz (175g) Gruyère cheese, grated
2oz (50g) parmesan, grated
salt and black pepper
10 sheets filo pastry
2oz (50g) unsalted butter, melted

Sweat the onion, garlic and leeks in a pan in the olive oil until soft.

Cook the spinach in a pan in very little water for 3–5 minutes. Drain well and press out any excess liquid. Allow to cool slightly.

Stir in the breadcrumbs, onion and leek mixture, together with the beaten eggs. Add the three cheeses and season well with salt and pepper.

Use half the filo pastry sheets to line an 8–9in spring-clip tin, brushing melted butter between each layer of pastry.

Spoon the spinach and cheese filling into the pastry case, placing the remaining pastry sheets on top. Fold the edges of the lower sheets over the top sheets and brush the top with the remaining butter.

Bake at 375°F/190°C/Gas 5 for 25–30 minutes, or until the pie is golden-brown.

SALMON AND WATERCRESS PARCELS WITH SORREL SAUCE

SERVES 4

'I can't think of anything easier to make that's more delicious, and I just adore salmon. If it's difficult to find sorrel – I grow it, of course – use some small spinach leaves,' suggested Lynda.

4 medium pieces of salmon fillet, approx 6oz (175g) each
1 small bunch watercress
2oz (50g) melted butter
grated rind of ½ lemon
salt
freshly ground black pepper
1pkt (400g) filo pastry (8 sheets– square ones are best. Trim large sheets as necessary to make neat parcels)
4tbsp soured cream

FOR THE SAUCE

4 spring onions, finely chopped
4fl oz (100ml) dry white wine
5fl oz (142ml) thick double cream
4oz (100g) sorrel or small spinach leaves, finely shredded
a few sprigs parsley and tarragon

Remove carefully any fine bones and skin from the salmon.

Rinse the watercress, discarding any tough stems, and dry on kitchen paper. Chop finely.

Mix the lemon rind and salt and pepper into the cream.

Brush 4 sheets of filo with melted butter, top each with a second sheet and brush again. Place a piece of salmon fillet on each. Scatter the watercress on the salmon and top with a tablespoon of the seasoned sour cream. Gather the pastry up around the fish to make parcels, and place on a baking sheet. Brush the parcels with the remaining melted butter.

Bake in a preheated oven at 375°F/190°C/Gas 5 for about 20 minutes, or until the pastry is crisp and golden.

To make the sauce, cook the chopped spring onions gently in the white wine until the wine is reduced by half. Add the cream and heat gently until boiling and slightly thickened. Add the shredded sorrel leaves and chopped parsley and tarragon. Season with salt and white or lemon pepper.

Blend to a purée in a liquidiser or food processor. Reheat and keep the sauce warm until required.

ELDERFLOWER PÉTILLANT

Fun to make and even more fun to drink, this is so lively and potent you need to recork it once a day! To stop the constant popping Robert expertly wires the corks in place.

12 large heads of elderflowers in full bloom
rind and juice of 2 lemons
4.5L (1 gallon) fresh spring water
1lb (450g) granulated sugar
3–4tbsp white wine vinegar

Shake and rinse the flower heads to remove any insects.

Immerse the elderflowers in the cold spring water and add the sugar, vinegar and lemon rind and juice. Leave for 48 hours.

Strain the liquid carefully through a muslin cloth.

Bottle and cork, storing in a cool place for 2 weeks before using.

COURGETTE FLOWER FRITTERS

SERVES 6 AS A STARTER

'You must gather the flowers in the morning with the dew still on them before the morning sun can wilt them.' Lynda serves this starter when her courgette harvest is at its height. 'It's always a conversation stopper' she crows.

3oz (75g) plain flour
a pinch of salt
1tbsp corn oil
5fl oz (150ml/ ¼pt) water, or less
1 medium size egg white
12–18 courgette flowers
olive oil for frying

Sift the flour and salt together. Add the corn oil and water and beat until smooth. Allow this to stand for an hour.

Beat the egg white until stiff and fold it into the creamy-textured batter with a metal spoon.

Carefully remove the stamens from each courgette flower without spoiling their shape, and wipe the flowers with a damp cloth. Dip each flower into the batter and fry for 2–3 minutes in olive oil until golden brown, turning halfway through cooking.

Drain on kitchen paper and bring the fritters to the table as soon as possible to enjoy the crispness and delectable flavour.

Serve either with lemon wedges, a tomato coulis or dusted lightly with parmesan cheese.

COUNTRY · CUTTINGS

Add snipped sun-dried tomatoes or olives to bread dough before shaping into interesting and unusual loaves or rolls.

Lynda says, 'Do you realise vinegar gets its name from *vin aigre* or sour wine. So why not use lemon juice as a gentle substitute in French dressing?'

SPRING NETTLE SOUP

SERVES 4–6

There are not many nettles to be found in the grounds of Ambridge Hall according to Lynda Snell, but she manages to pick the fresh young nettle tops from the clumps very close to Bridge Farm. 'At least you know they've not been sprayed there,' she said.

1lb (450g) young nettles
3oz (75g) butter
4oz (100g) potatoes, peeled and diced
4oz (100g) spring onions, trimmed and chopped
30fl oz (900ml/1½pt) chicken stock (or use a stock cube)
2oz (50g) watercress, rinsed
sea salt and freshly ground black pepper
10fl oz (275ml/ ½pt) single cream

Wearing rubber gloves, snip the tops from the young nettles, then rinse and chop them well.

Melt the butter in a large saucepan over a low heat, stir in the potatoes and spring onions, cover the pan and simmer gently for 10 minutes.

Stir in the nettles and add the stock. Bring to the boil and simmer for 20 minutes. Add the watercress to the pan for the final 2 minutes.

Cool slightly then purée in a blender or food processor. Return to the rinsed pan, season and stir in the cream. Reheat for 1 or 2 minutes taking care that it does not boil.

BRUSCHETTE WITH GOAT'S CHEESE AND BASIL

SERVES 4–6

Robert admits this is a favourite light supper snack in front of the television. But Lynda's furious if the crumbs are dropped on the Chinese rug!

1 flat rustic-style country loaf (or an Italian ciabatta)
1 plump garlic clove
4tbsp extra virgin olive oil
6oz (175g) fresh goat's-milk cheese
a bunch of fresh basil leaves

Split the loaf horizontally and cut into 2in strips. Arrange on a baking sheet and grill the slices, inner surface uppermost, until they are just starting to brown.

Crush the garlic cloves into the olive oil and, while the bread is still warm, brush the top of the strips generously with oil and top with slices of goat's cheese.

Place under a hot grill briefly before serving. Decorate with basil leaves.

TOMATO COULIS

SERVES 6

'I just close my eyes and dream I'm in the Mediterranean when I smell this cooking,' Lynda remarks.

½ Spanish onion, finely chopped
2tbsp olive oil
1lb (450g) ripe tomatoes, skinned, deseeded and chopped
1 garlic clove, finely chopped
a pinch of brown sugar
1 bunch of fresh herbs, containing a bay leaf, a sprig of parsley, thyme and marjoram

Soften the onion in the olive oil over a low heat and add the tomatoes, garlic, sugar and herbs. Cover and cook gently for 30 minutes.

When you have a thick pulp, remove the herbs and cool the mixture. Purée the sauce for a finer consistency if preferred.

Always make more tomato coulis than you need and freeze the remainder in small tubs – ideal for adding to numerous savoury dishes.

GOOSEBERRY SORBET

SERVES 6

A sharp refreshing sorbet to cleanse the palate. It is particularly attractive when made with pink gooseberries. Lynda thinks it 'de rigueur' to serve it between a rich starter and the main course.

12oz (350g) gooseberries
8oz (225g) caster sugar
grated rind and juice of 1 lemon
20fl oz (600ml/1pt) water
2 medium size egg whites

Rinse the gooseberries thoroughly but do not top and tail them. Place them in a pan with the sugar, lemon rind and juice and water. Bring this slowly to the boil and simmer for 10 minutes. Then pass the cooked fruit through a sieve and allow to cool.

Whisk the egg whites until stiff and beat them into the purée. Place in a freezer container and freeze for 2–3 hours, or until almost solid.

Remove from the freezer and beat thoroughly to break down the ice crystals. Return to the freezer for 1–2 hours until completely set.

MUSKY MULBERRY AND HAZELNUT ROULADE

SERVES 6–8

Robert absolutely adores this dessert served with glossy chocolate sauce. Too rich for me though – and thinking about those extra inches I'd rather make a sharp mulberry coulis.

4 medium size eggs
4oz (100g) caster sugar
3oz (75g) ground toasted hazelnuts
1tsp baking powder
a little icing sugar
6fl oz (175ml) double cream
2tbsp framboise liqueur (optional)
8oz (225g) fresh mulberries, and a few for decoration, or fresh or frozen raspberries

Grease a 12 × 8in Swiss roll tin and line with baking parchment.

Whisk the eggs and sugar in a bowl placed over a pan of hot water, until pale and thick. Gently fold in the ground toasted hazelnuts and sifted baking powder. Spread the mixture in the prepared tin and bake for 15 minutes at 400°F/200°C/Gas 6. Then allow the cake to cool.

Place a piece of greaseproof paper dredged with icing sugar on the work surface. Turn out the cake, having loosened the edges first, and trim off the crisp edges.

Whip the cream until stiff, gradually adding the liqueur, and then spread it over the cake with a palette knife.

Scatter some of the mulberries over, then, using the greaseproof paper to help, roll up the cake like a Swiss roll.

Don't worry if the surface of the roulade cracks – it actually adds to the delicious home-made appearance.

Transfer to a serving dish. Decorate with the reserved mulberries and dredge with icing sugar. Chill in the fridge for at least 2 hours before serving.

CHOCOLATE SAUCE

4oz (100g) good quality plain chocolate
3tbsp golden syrup
3fl oz (90ml) single cream

Break the chocolate into pieces and melt over a bowl of hot water. Stir in the syrup.

Heat the cream without boiling and gradually stir into the chocolate mixture. Flood plate with sauce and place the roulade on top, if making a big impression.

MULBERRY COULIS

12oz (350g) fresh mulberries (or fresh or frozen raspberries)
5oz (150g) caster sugar
juice of ½ small lemon
1tbsp brandy

Put all the ingredients into a blender or food processor. Blend together, then rub through a fine sieve. Chill before serving.

MIDSUMMER PUDDING

SERVES 6

Having frozen a mélange of midsummer fruits, Lynda likes nothing better than to astonish her guests with this pudding in the depths of winter. It conjures up the magic of those warm evenings – she and Robert sitting under the cream canvas of their colonial sunshade sipping chilled Chardonnay.

1½lb (675g) mixed red fruits, preferably strawberries, raspberries and redcurrants
4oz (100g) soft light brown sugar
8–10 thin slices of 2-day-old white bread, crusts removed (or to be extra special, bread made with egg eg brioche or rich French bread)

Prepare the fruit, rinse and place in a heavy-bottomed saucepan. Add the sugar and heat gently for 5–8 minutes.

Line a 1½pt pudding basin with the sliced bread, cutting a circle of bread to fit the base.

When the fruit is cooked pour it carefully into the basin, reserving about 6tbsp of the syrup. When the basin is full, top with a layer of bread. Lay a plate or saucer that just fits inside the rim on top of the pudding, and place a weight on top of that. Leave overnight in the fridge.

To serve, run a knife around the edge to loosen and turn the pudding on to a serving dish. Spoon over the remaining fruit juice and serve with dollops of crème fraîche or Greek yogurt.

COUNTRY · CUTTINGS

Lynda serves iced tea combined with ginger ale for a refreshing summer drink. She pours the tea over ice, adds sugar and tops with ginger ale. Add a squeeze of lemon or lime juice to taste.

Lynda folds calendula petals (marigold) into whipped cream, first breaking off the little white heel.

THE LODGE

IT'S ABSOLUTELY CLEAR. Look, there it is in black and white, over across Arkwright Lake and away beyond Jack's flowering chestnuts. Surely you can make out its neat and chequered shape tucked in at the hem of the country park? It's really charming now, sitting prettily in its prim and pristine patch of closely shorn lawn, sheltered by bramble and tangle-free trees and Eddie's macheted shrubbery. Perfectly secluded, it is overlooked only by the goddess of gardens and love, the faintly smiling Aphrodite.

Just how did Mum cope with the sanding, plastering, painting and staining? And with Jason moaning and whistling all the time .

Now in the autumn of their years, Peggy and Jack can sit in cushioned comfort surveying their new-found and more distant vista, while the pale yellow sun casts long shafts of colour on smiling Aphrodite and the wall-to-wall Wilton in the hall.

STEAK, KIDNEY AND MUSHROOM PUDDING

SERVES 4–6

'Ooh, Peggy, that succulent gravy and puffy crust! What have I been missing all these years?' enthuses Jack as he licks his lips.

1lb (450g) best stewing steak, trimmed of excess fat
4oz (100g) lamb's kidney, skinned, cored and cubed
2tbsp flour
salt and pepper
3tbsp oil
1 large onion, chopped
6oz (175g) button mushrooms, thickly sliced
3 pickled walnuts, diced
6fl oz (175ml) beef stock

FOR THE SUET CRUST PASTRY
8oz (225g) plain or self-raising flour
½tsp salt
½tsp baking powder
3oz (75g) shredded suet
1tbsp horseradish sauce
about 4fl oz (100ml) water

To make the filling, cut the steak into 1in cubes. Toss the steak and kidney in the flour and season with salt and pepper. Heat the oil in a frying pan and add the meat to the pan, frying in small batches. When browned remove to a casserole dish.

Fry the onion until lightly brown and transfer to the casserole, adding the mushrooms, walnuts and stock.

Cover the casserole and simmer on a low heat or in a slow oven (325°F/160°C/Gas 3) for an hour. Allow to cool.

To make the crust pastry, sieve the flour, salt and baking powder into a bowl. Stir in the suet and the horseradish sauce and mix to a soft dough with cold water.

Turn on to a floured board and knead until smooth. Then roll out two-thirds of the dough and line a 2pt pudding basin.

Spoon the meat and gravy into the suet-lined basin. Roll out a pastry lid from the remains of the suet crust, moisten the edges and press firmly down to seal. Cover with a lid of greaseproof paper and foil, both pleated to allow room for the crust to rise. Steam or boil steadily for 2½–3 hours, remembering to top up the water level from time to time.

BUTTERED CARAWAY CABBAGE

SERVES 4–6

As a child I just did not like caraway seeds – maybe they are an acquired taste.

1½lb (675g) white cabbage
5fl oz (150ml/ ¼pt) salted water
bay leaf
2oz (50g) butter
1tsp caraway seeds
salt and black pepper

Shred the cabbage finely, steam or boil in the salted water with the bay leaf, until the cabbage is cooked but still quite crisp. Drain well and discard the bay leaf.

Melt the butter in the pan, add the cabbage and reheat. Sprinkle on the caraway seeds and freshly ground black pepper, tossing the mixture with a spaghetti fork. Serve at once.

COUNTRY·CUTTINGS

Granny Perkins often added cold coffee instead of milk to steamed chocolate or ginger puddings.

Make your own special gentleman's relish by combining a tin of anchovies with grated lemon rind. Pound, in a mortar, adding a little vinegar and black pepper. Heat gently in a small pan. Pack in a small dish and refrigerate.

Aunt Laura's cure for creaking joints – Boil 2lb (1kg) chopped celery in 80fl oz (2.3L/4pt) water until tender. Add 1½lb (675g) brown sugar and ¼oz (5g) yeast, and then bottle.

TREACLE, LEMON AND GINGER TART

SERVES 4–6

A typical English pudding. Conn, my mother's visiting American friend, was entranced by it – as well as by her! 'Sure is real good. Better than Pecan Pie,' he drawled.

6oz (175g) plain flour
½tsp ground ginger
pinch of salt
3oz (75g) butter or hard margarine
cold water to mix

2oz (50g) fresh white breadcrumbs
½tsp ground ginger
juice of ½ lemon
8oz (225g) golden syrup
grated rind of 1 lemon
1tbsp demerara sugar

Sift the flour, ½tsp of ginger and salt into a bowl. Rub in the butter until it resembles fine breadcrumbs. Add the cold water to mix to a stiff dough and knead until smooth. Wrap in foil and chill in the fridge for half an hour.

Roll the pastry out on a floured surface and line an 8in fluted flan dish. Reserve the pastry trimmings.

Prick the base of the tart and sprinkle on the breadcrumbs, ½tsp of ginger and lemon rind. Pour on the syrup and lemon juice – the syrup will spread itself over the crumbs. Sprinkle with demerara sugar and decorate the top with a lattice of pastry strips.

Bake in a moderately hot oven at 400°F/200°C/Gas 6 for 25 minutes or until the pastry is golden.

COUNTRY·CUTTINGS

Instead of putting a lemon in a Sussex Pond Pudding, Peggy puts small kumquats, pricked all over, in her suet pastry lined basin for her Borset Pond Pudding.

BREAD AND BUTTER PUDDING

SERVES 4

'We don't eat much bread, me and Jack, so this is a good way of using up the remainder of the loaf.'

If the eggs are separated and the whites folded in later, the pudding will be almost soufflé-like.

6 thin slices of white bread, crusts removed
2oz (50g) butter
2tbsp marmalade
2oz (50g) currants
2 whole eggs and 1 egg yolk
20fl oz (600ml/1pt) milk
grated rind of 1 lemon
2oz (50g) demerara sugar
1tsp cinnamon

Spread the bread slices with butter and marmalade and cut into triangles. Grease a 2pt pudding basin and arrange the bread in layers, sprinkling each layer with the currants, and finishing with a layer of bread.

Beat the eggs and milk together, add the grated lemon rind and pour over the bread. Leave to stand for an hour.

Sprinkle the top of the pudding with the sugar and the cinnamon before baking in a preheated oven at 325°F/160°C/Gas 3 for 50–60 minutes. The top should be crusty and golden brown. Serve with cream or custard.

GRANNY PERKINS' LEMON PUDDING

SERVES 4–6

'Nobody ever makes this as well as your Gran did,' Mum said wistfully.

The top of the pudding should be crisp and golden, while underneath is a smooth and lemony sauce.

3oz (75g) butter or margarine
4oz (100g) caster sugar
juice and rind of 2 small lemons
2oz (50g) plain flour
½tsp baking powder
2 medium eggs (separated)
5fl oz (150ml/ ¼pt) milk

Cream the butter and sugar with the grated lemon rind until light and fluffy. Fold in the sifted flour and baking powder. Add the egg yolks only and whisk together with the lemon juice and milk.

Beat the egg whites stiffly until standing in peaks and fold into the lemon mixture.

Bake in a buttered 6in soufflé dish placed within a baking tin half-filled with water, for 40 minutes at 350°F/180°C/Gas 4.

Serve immediately, preferably with whipped cream.

GOOSEBERRY FOOL

SERVES 6

Gooseberries were a favourite fruit in the nineteenth century, and even now prove to be a popular dessert for a warm July day.

1lb (450g) ripe gooseberries, topped and tailed
6oz (175g) caster sugar
2 elderflower heads (optional)
8fl oz (225ml) double cream, whipped
grated rind of 1 small orange

Put the gooseberries and sugar in a pan, cover and simmer for 10–15 minutes until tender. (One or two heads of elderflower, tied in a muslin cloth, can be boiled with the gooseberries to counteract the acidity.) Allow to cool.

Put through a blender or rub through a sieve. Then fold in the cream and grated orange rind.

Spoon into individual dishes, chill and serve with wafer-thin biscuits.

NELSON'S WINE BAR

'A FASHIONABLE SLICE OF BORSETSHIRE *society please, followed by the crème de la crème, vin de Vivaldi or a chilled glass of Gershwin,' I heard myself say as I sank down, gratefully stretching my weary limbs in ratan-seated reverie. Soporifically soothed by the civilised chink of china and Nelson's seductively louche and cynical charm, I was relieved to have escaped from the hustle of Borchester's market madness to this art deco oasis. Shane's shadowy figure bobbed behind striped terrines and tureens of steaming soup, the exotic smells enticing me with peppery pâtés and piquant pies.*

Nelson raised a quizzical eyebrow. 'Jennifer, my dear, would you kindly mind repeating that?'

'Oh, an unfashionable slice of Shane's Borsetshire quiche please Nelson, followed by lemon crème brûlée, vin de table or a glass of Chardonnay!'

STILTON, CELERY AND PEAR SOUP

SERVES 4–6

'Why do you think this is on the menu in January, Jennifer – what else could we do with the Christmas Stilton?' Nelson asked drolly.

1oz (25g) butter or margarine
1 medium onion, finely chopped
3 celery sticks, finely chopped
1tbsp plain flour
1 wineglass dry white wine
20fl oz (600ml/1pt) chicken stock
10fl oz (275ml/½pt) milk
1 large ripe pear (William or Conference), peeled and chopped
salt and pepper
4oz (100g) Stilton cheese

Melt the butter in a saucepan, add the onion and celery and cook gently until soft. Stir in the flour and cook for one minute. Gradually add the wine and stock, and stir until thickened and smooth. Add the milk, pear and seasoning. Cover and simmer for about 20 minutes.

Crumble in the Stilton and stir until melted. Adjust the seasoning and serve piping hot.

SHANE'S SMOOTH AVOCADO SOUP

SERVES 6

I remarked to Nelson that this was an excellent way of using avocados slightly too discoloured for serving au naturel. *'Don't give away all our secrets', he hissed.*

1oz (25g) butter
1 medium onion, finely chopped
1lb (450g) sweet potatoes, peeled and diced
30fl oz (900ml/1½pt) chicken or vegetable stock
grated rind and juice of 1 orange and 1 lemon
2 ripe avocados
a dash of tabasco sauce
a pinch of mace, salt and pepper

Melt the butter in a large saucepan over a low heat and fry the onion and potatoes gently for 4–6 minutes. Add the stock and bring to the boil. Cover and simmer for 20 minutes. Then add the zest of the whole orange and that of half the lemon and the juice of both.

Halve the avocados, discard the stones and chop into pieces. Add to the soup mixture with the tabasco and seasoning. Purée the mixture in a blender or food processor.

Serve hot with croutons, or cold with a whirl of single cream.

BRANDIED CHICKEN PÂTÉ

SERVES 8–10

Shane says, 'If you prefer a really smooth pâté, put the meats through a food processor or blender. It must be served with really hot, crisp brown toast'.

12oz (350g) chicken liver
6oz (175g) cooked bacon or ham
12oz (350g) pork sausage meat
2 cloves garlic, crushed
1tsp thyme
1tsp mushroom ketchup
2tsp brandy
salt and pepper
8oz (225g) streaky bacon
2 bay leaves
parsley sprigs to garnish

Clean the chicken livers and mince them together with the ham. Add the sausage meat, crushed garlic, thyme, mushroom ketchup, brandy and seasoning, mixing well.

Line a terrine or pâté dish with the streaky bacon and fill with the meat mixture. Top with bacon rashers and bay leaves.

Cover with foil and place in a baking tin half-filled with water, and cook at 350°F/180°C/Gas 4 for about 1½ hours.

Garnish with parsley sprigs, and serve with crisp brown toast or crusty bread, and farm-house butter.

ASPARAGUS AND HAM QUICHE

SERVES 6

One of Shane's popular quiches, though Nelson wonders why it's still on the menu. I must admit I think it much more exciting made with fresh asparagus.

6oz (175g) shortcrust pastry
10oz (275g) can asparagus tips
4oz (100g) chopped ham
10fl oz (275ml/ ½pt) single cream
2 large size eggs
salt and black pepper

Line a 9in fluted flan tin with the pastry. Prick the bottom lightly with a fork. Trim the asparagus into 1in pieces and arrange in the base of the flan with the chopped ham.

Beat together the cream, eggs and seasoning and pour over the ham and asparagus.

Bake in a hot oven at 400°F/200°C/Gas 6 for 15 minutes, then reduce the heat to 350°F/180°C/Gas 4 and cook for a further 20 minutes, until the filling is set and golden brown.

Serve hot or cold.

QUICHE AUX FRUITS DE MER

SERVES 6

An excellent savoury tart for a light lunch or supper. Serve hot or cold with a crispy green salad in a lemony dressing.

6oz (175g) shortcrust pastry
2tbsp chopped shallots
1½oz (40g) butter
4oz (100g) prawns, fresh or frozen
2oz (50g) tinned crabmeat
2tbsp white wine
salt and black pepper
3 medium size eggs
6fl oz (175ml) single cream
1tbsp tomato purée
1oz (25g) Gruyère cheese, grated

Roll out the pastry and line a 9in fluted flan tin.

Cook the shallots in the butter until soft and transparent. Add the prawns and crabmeat and stir gently for 2 minutes. Add the wine and seasoning and heat gently until bubbling.

Beat the eggs together with the cream and tomato purée and gradually blend into the shellfish mixture. Adjust the seasoning. Pour the mixture into the flan tin and sprinkle the Gruyère cheese over it.

Bake in a preheated oven at 375°F/190°C/Gas 5 for 25–30 minutes until puffy and brown.

COUNTRY · CUTTINGS

Creamy mashed potato is made especially good and given a touch of sophistication by sieving the boiled potato and mixing with thick yogurt and crushed garlic.

HERBED AND CHEESY BREAD

SERVES 4–6

Served with a side salad this makes a filling snack – let's not add up the calories!

1 long or 2 short French bread sticks
4oz (100g) slightly salted softened butter
2 fat cloves garlic, crushed
1tbsp chopped fresh chives and parsley
6oz (175g) grated cheddar cheese
black pepper

Cut vertical slits in the bread at about 1in intervals, taking care not to cut right through.

In a bowl mix the butter, garlic, herbs, half the grated cheese and freshly ground pepper.

Spread the mixture between each slice of the bread and wrap in foil to completely enclose the loaf.

Bake in a preheated oven at 400°F/200°C/Gas 6 for 15 minutes. Then open the foil and sprinkle with the remaining cheese, returning to the oven for 5 minutes, or until the cheese has melted. Serve hot.

BRIE AND WALNUT TART

SERVES 6

This is Elizabeth's favourite and when served straight from the oven the filling is light and soufflé-like.

FOR THE PASTRY

6oz (175g) plain white flour
pinch of salt
3oz (75g) butter or margarine
1 medium size egg yolk
water to mix

FOR THE FILLING

6oz (175g) Brie cheese
juice of ½ lemon
2oz (50g) chopped walnuts
3 medium size eggs
10fl oz (275ml) single cream
salt and pepper

To prepare the shortcrust pastry, sieve the flour and salt into a mixing bowl. Cut the butter into cubes and rub lightly into the flour with the fingertips until it resembles fine breadcrumbs.

Beat the egg yolk with a little water and mix into the flour with a knife to make a soft dough.

Turn on to a floured surface and roll out to the required thickness. Line a 9in flan tin with the pastry and bake blind in a moderately hot oven 375–400°F/190–200°C/Gas 5–6 for 15–20 minutes.

For the filling, soak the sliced Brie in lemon juice for half an hour. Place the cheese and the walnuts in the base of the flan case. Whisk the eggs and cream together and season well. Pour into the flan and bake in a preheated oven at 325°F/160°C/Gas 3 for 45 minutes, or until the filling is light and puffy and browned.

COUNTRY · CUTTINGS

Pulverise rose petals or lavender flowers in an electric grinder. Add the powder with the sugar when making meringues for a new and delicious flavour.

BAKED APRICOT CHEESECAKE

SERVES 6–8

This is a sumptuous cake to complement a mid-morning cup of coffee, especially when served with a dollop of cream whipped together with apricot brandy.

4oz (100g) dried apricots
3oz (75g) butter
4oz (100g) caster sugar
rind and juice of 1 lemon
10oz (275g) cream cheese
2 medium size eggs, separated
2oz (50g) ground almonds
1oz (25g) ground rice
a little icing sugar

Soak the apricots overnight if necessary. Chop them coarsely.

Cream the butter, sugar and lemon rind together until pale and light. Add the sieved cream cheese and egg yolks, beating thoroughly. Stir in the ground almonds, ground rice, lemon juice and chopped apricots.

Whisk the egg whites until stiff and fold into the cheese mixture.

Turn into a greased and lined 8in loose-bottomed cake tin and bake at 350°F/180°C/Gas 4 for 50–60 minutes.

Turn off the heat and leave the cheesecake to cool slowly in the oven.

ST STEPHEN'S SUMMER FÊTE

'DARLING, DON'T BE SILLY, you can't wear a duffle coat.' But Alice was adamant – and also about her marmalade sandwiches.

I stared distractedly at the tightly packed pages of my leather-bound engagement book. It was midsummer's social madness! Wide-brimmed hats and umbrellas at Ascot; stiff straw boaters and hampers at Henley with iced Pimm's at picnics; a last minute decision in favour of a smidgeon of smoked salmon, a singles match and a strawberry or two at Wimbledon; and that tiringly crowded round of arenas at the Royal.

Now it's the post-shearing, pre-harvesting, most suitable Saturday in July, dawning fresh and breezily bright. 'A thin band of cloud will move slowly south throughout the day.'

Marjorie Antrobus cheerfully exercised her boisterous hounds, then changed into her, hopefully, crumple-free cream linen suit, decidedly colonial skewbald shoes and a floppy calico-coloured chipper panama, last worn for polo (chukkas viewed in the shade of Teddy's Kenyan clubhouse). It would be ideal for the ear-piercing opening of the Ambridge village fête on the platform at 2.30. 'It gives me great pleasure to see . . .'

Multi-coloured flags and bunting fluttered over the stalls on the village green. Gold-braided, brass-buttoned George Barford, his collar too tight, puffed in the massed ranks of the Hollerton Town Band, triple-tongueing his silver cornet with unrehearsed alacrity.

Robert Snell sits, obsequiously efficient, at the gate attending to the ticket counting, while sequin-lidded Lynda, in the guise of Madame Za Za, lures unsuspecting victims to her tarot telling.

Tony Archer, swilling beer, oversees the wooden ball-throwing for hairy coconuts and pink pigs, while pinafore'd Phil and Brian manfully tend the hissing chromium urn in the crowded tea tent. Booted and jodhpured Kate and Christine are waved goodbye by countless proud mothers, as plump and placid ponies are led round the green with their tearful little charges.

'How many sweeties are in my jar?' asks innocent imp-like Edward Grundy, with a sticky grin.

'Borchester Weight-watchers' membership doubles!' is the headline in the next edition of the Echo, *as the WI Cake Stall is cleared of all but crumbs and a few overdone buns in a matter of minutes.*

A dark band of gathering cloud moves ominously closer and large drops of rain begin to fall. 'The judging of the children's fancy dress will now take place.' Marjorie Antrobus, in her shrinking and embarrassingly clinging linen suit, pins a 'third' on Little Bo-Peep, drenched in sprig-muslin but still clutching her wet and woolly sheep. A 'second' certificate she hands to Little Miss Muffet on her soaked tuffet. But the well-earned first prize goes to Alice Aldridge, piously smiling and suitably clad in a duffle coat, shiny oilskin sou'wester and bright blue waterproof boots – still looking after Paddington Bear's specially spread marmalade sandwiches.

A DATE FOR YOUR DIARY

This year's SUMMER FETE will be held on July 14th at 2.30 p.m. on the Village Green. We are delighted to announce that Mrs. Marjorie Antrobus has kindly agreed to perform the opening ceremony.
HOLLERTON TOWN BAND will entertain and there will be Pony Rides, Bowling for the Pig, Fortune Telling and all the usual stalls - and of course - don't forget - CHILDREN'S FANCY DRESS.
All cakes for the Cake Stall should be delivered to Mrs. Jill Archer in good time.

WALTER GABRIEL'S GINGERNUTS

MAKES ABOUT 24

Granny P used to make these specially for dear old Uncle Walter. He would dunk them slyly in his tea when he thought she wasn't looking.

4oz (100g) butter or margarine
1tbsp golden syrup
3oz (75g) brown sugar
6oz (175g) self-raising flour
1tsp bicarbonate of soda
1tsp ground ginger
pinch of salt

Put the butter, syrup and sugar together in a pan and melt over a low heat.

Sift together the flour, bicarbonate of soda, ginger and salt, and add these to the melted ingredients in the pan, stirring thoroughly.

Place the mixture in small heaps on a greased baking tray and flatten slightly. Bake for 10–15 minutes at 375°F/190°C/Gas 5 until golden brown.

PAT ARCHER'S APRICOT YOGURT SCONES

MAKES 10–12

These are Tommy's favourites, especially when he's raced back home from the school bus, ravenous as usual. He loves them warm and spread with butter.

8oz (225g) self-raising flour (half white, half wholewheat)
pinch of salt
1oz (25g) caster sugar
2oz (50g) lard
2oz (50g) chopped dried apricots (ready-soaked)
6fl oz (175ml) apricot yogurt

Sift the flour, salt and sugar together. Rub in the lard and then add the chopped apricots. Mix in the yogurt to form a soft dough, adding a little milk if the mixture is too stiff.

Roll the mixture out on a floured board and cut into rounds with a pastry cutter.

Brush with milk and place on a greased baking tray, and bake in a hot oven at 425°F/220°C/Gas 7 for about 10 minutes or until golden-brown.

BAKER'S FLOOR CAKE

Rumour has it that this was the cake made from the sweepings at the end of the day in Doughy Hood's bakehouse.

2oz (50g) chopped walnuts
2oz (50g) chopped dates
2oz (50g) halved cherries
1oz (25g) mixed peel
2 medium size eggs
4oz (100g) self-raising flour
5oz (150g) sugar
a pinch of cinnamon and mixed spice

Mix all the fruit together in a bowl with the beaten eggs. Add the sifted flour, sugar and spices and beat together thoroughly.

Spread the mixture into a greased, lined Swiss roll tin (approximately 7 × 11in) and bake at 350°F/180°C/Gas 4 for 40 minutes.

MARJORIE'S MARMALADE CAKE

Mrs Antrobus has often been seen on her way to the Vicarage to take Robin a freshly baked cake. Coals to Newcastle, I would have thought.

6oz (175g) butter
6oz (175g) soft brown sugar
grated rind and juice of 1 medium orange
3 medium size eggs
2tbsp chunky marmalade
7oz (200g) self-raising flour
1tsp mixed spice
4oz (100g) mixed fruit

Cream together the butter, sugar and orange rind until fluffy. Add the beaten eggs and the marmalade. Fold in the sifted flour and spice. Add the mixed fruit and orange juice and combine thoroughly.

Turn the mixture into a lined and greased 7in cake tin and bake at 350°F/180°C/Gas 4 for 1¼ hours. Leave to cool in the tin before turning out.

COUNTRY·CUTTINGS

Betty Tucker says she makes her fruit cakes moist by adding a tablespoon of marmalade in preference to chopped candied peel.

Auntie Pru said use a wooden spoon to stir the jam; and cane sugar is better than beet sugar for jam-making.

PAT'S ALMOND LOAF

There are always eggs and yogurt in abundance at Bridge Farm. This tea-time treat makes good use of these, and is perfect for offering to visiting family and friends with an afternoon mug of tea.

½tsp bicarbonate of soda
5fl oz (150ml/ ¼pt) plain yogurt
4oz (100g) butter or margarine
4oz (100g) caster sugar
2 large size eggs, separated
1tsp almond essence
6oz (175g) self-raising flour
2oz (50g) ground almonds

FOR THE TOPPING
3tbsp icing sugar
3–4tbsp hot water
1tsp flaked and toasted almonds

Add the bicarbonate of soda to the yogurt, mix well and set to one side.

Grease and line a 2lb loaf tin.

Cream the butter and sugar until pale and fluffy. Add the beaten egg yolks and almond essence, then fold in the flour, ground almonds and yogurt.

Whisk the egg whites until stiff but not dry, then fold into the cake mixture. Put into the loaf tin.

Bake in the centre of the oven at 350°F/180°C/Gas 4 for 50–60 minutes, then turn out on to a wire rack to cool.

To make the topping, mix the icing sugar with the water and spread over the top of the cake. Sprinkle with the almonds.

MRS HORROBIN'S OAT CRUNCHIES

MAKES 12–16

It's very kind of the Horrobins – and unusual too – to give anything to the fête. (I should think she's almost the only person in the village who still uses lard.)

3oz (75g) caster sugar
2oz (50g) lard
2oz (50g) margarine or butter
3tsp boiling water
1tsp golden syrup
a few drops of almond essence
2oz (50g) oats
4oz (100g) self-raising flour

Cream the sugar, lard and margarine together in a bowl. When pale and fluffy, beat in the hot water, syrup and almond essence. Then stir in the oats and flour and mix together thoroughly.

Take teaspoons of the mixture and roll into walnut-sized balls, and place on a greased baking tray. Leave space for the biscuits to spread.

Bake at 350°F/180°C/Gas 4 for 10–15 minutes. Allow to cool on a wire rack.

FREDA FRY'S VICTORIAN FAIRINGS

MAKES ABOUT 24

These are made as they were for fairs in Victorian times, according to Bert's wife . . . and who am I to argue?

4oz (100g) margarine or butter
1tbsp syrup
3oz (75g) brown sugar
6oz (175g) self-raising flour
½tsp bicarbonate of soda
1tsp ground ginger
½tsp ground mixed spice
pinch of salt

Melt the butter and syrup in a pan over a low heat and stir in the sugar. Remove from the heat and add the sieved flour, soda, spices and salt. Mix until a soft and smooth dough is formed.

Take rounded teaspoons of the mixture, roll into balls and place on greased baking trays, leaving room for the biscuits to spread.

Bake at 350°F/180°C/Gas 4 for 10–15 minutes and then allow to cool on a wire rack.

WALNUT BREAD

There's nothing to compare with Pat's Walnut Bread served warm with a chunk of crumbly Borsetshire cheese. This recipe could also be used to make three round loaves. Place them on baking sheets and cook for 30–35 minutes.

1oz (25g) fresh yeast or 1tbsp easy-blend dried yeast
½tsp honey
1pt (550ml) approx warm water
2½lb (1.125kg) strong wholemeal flour
2tsp salt
8fl oz (225ml/ ½pt) plain yogurt
4oz (100g) chopped walnuts

In a small bowl mix the yeast, honey and a little tepid water. In a large bowl mix together the flour and salt. Make a well in the middle of the flour, add the yeast, yogurt and warm water and mix to a soft dough.

Turn on to a floured surface and knead until the dough is smooth and elastic. Prove the dough in a covered bowl in a warm place for 1–1½ hours, until doubled in size. (This first proving should be omitted if using easy-blend dried yeast.) Then, divide the dough into two and knead lightly, working half the chopped walnuts with each piece of dough, and place into two 1½lb greased loaf tins. Cover with a clean tea cloth and leave in a warm place to prove until doubled in size.

Bake the loaves at 425°F/220°C/Gas 7 for 45 minutes. When cooked, the loaves should sound hollow when tapped. Turn out and cool on a wire rack.

PEGGY ARCHER'S PASSION CAKE

A soft, moist carrot cake which can be eaten as a pudding too.

6fl oz (175ml) sunflower oil
6oz (175g) light soft brown sugar
3 medium eggs (size 3)
½tsp vanilla essence
8oz (225g) grated carrots
6oz (175g) unbleached self-raising flour
2oz (50g) ground almonds
1tsp ground cinnamon
½tsp ground nutmeg
½tsp salt
4oz (100g) raisins
4oz (100g) walnut pieces

FOR THE FROSTING
3oz (75g) cream cheese
2oz (50g) unsalted butter
4oz (100g) icing sugar
grated zest of 1 small orange

Grease and line a deep 8in cake tin.

Place the sunflower oil, sugar, eggs and vanilla essence in a bowl and beat well. Add the grated carrots and continue beating.

Place the remaining dry ingredients in another bowl and mix thoroughly. Then, together with the raisins and walnuts, add this dry mixture gradually to the carrot mixture.

Pour into the prepared tin and bake in the oven at 325°F/160°C/Gas 3 for about 1½ hours. Cover the top with foil if it browns too soon.

To make the frosting for the top of the cake, cream the cheese, butter and sugar together with the grated orange zest. Beat until smooth, then spread on the cake when it has cooled.

Make elderflower vinegar by steeping rinsed and shaken elderflowers in white wine vinegar, then strain through a muslin cloth.

AUNT LAURA'S BISCUITS

MAKES ABOUT 30

These crisp cookies are from New Zealand. Laura Archer must have passed her recipe on to Jill.

4oz (100g) butter
1tbsp golden syrup
8oz (225g) caster sugar
4oz (100g) desiccated coconut
4oz (100g) rolled oats
3oz (75g) plain flour
1tsp bicarbonate of soda
2tbsp water

In a saucepan melt the butter and syrup over a low heat. Allow to cool.

Mix together the sugar, coconut, oats and flour and gradually blend into the ingredients in the saucepan. Stir in the bicarbonate of soda and water.

Roll the mixture into walnut-sized balls, flatten slightly with a fork and place on greased baking sheets, well spaced out.

Bake at 350°F/180°C/Gas 4 for 20 minutes. Allow to cool before transferring to a wire tray.

MRS POTTER'S PEPPERMINT CREAMS

Manorfield Close is engulfed in peppermint creams at Christmas time. Good for the digestion.

1 medium size egg white
8oz (225g) icing sugar
1tsp peppermint essence
a few drops of green food colouring

In a bowl, beat the egg white until stiff. Add the sifted icing sugar. Beat in the peppermint essence until the mixture is a stiff, smooth paste, then drop in the green colouring and mix again.

Roll out on a board sprinkled with icing sugar. Cut out into rounds with a very small pastry cutter. Leave to set hard for 24 hours.

KATE'S COCONUT ICE

MAKES ABOUT 1½LB

Made somewhat grudgingly by my rather disgruntled daughter.

1lb (450g) granulated sugar
5fl oz (150ml/ ¼pt) milk
5oz (150g) desiccated coconut
pink food colouring

Put the sugar and milk into a large, thick-bottomed saucepan and bring to the boil. Boil gently for about 10 minutes. Remove the pan from the heat and stir in the coconut. Add drops of food colouring, stirring the mixture until the colour is pink enough for your liking.

Pour the mixture into a greased baking tin lined with greaseproof paper, and leave it in a cool place. When it has set, cut into squares and keep in an airtight container for up to a week.

CHOCOLATE CHERRY FUDGE

Chopped nuts can be used instead of cherries if you prefer.

4oz (100g) plain chocolate
4oz (100g) butter
3tbsp milk
1lb (450g) icing sugar, sifted
½tsp vanilla essence
4oz (100g) glacé cherries, chopped

Melt the chocolate and butter in a heavy saucepan over a low heat. Add the milk gradually, stirring all the time. Add the sifted icing sugar and boil gently until the mixture thickens.

Remove from the heat, add the vanilla flavouring and beat until the mixture becomes thick and creamy. Stir in the glacé cherries.

Pour into a buttered 8 × 6in tin and lightly mark into squares. Leave in the refrigerator for 1–2 hours until set, then cut into squares and store in an airtight container for 2–3 weeks.

THE VICARAGE

LONG GONE THE PEDAL-PUSHING PIETY of a dog-collared cleric living in the shabby splendour of draughty Georgian grandeur. The utilitarian, too dull to be deemed ugly vicarage, stands out as a silent, social comment on rural post-war architecture and, dare I say it, on our rural post-war vicar.

Having been involved in no small way with unfortunate Ms Bone (who had in turn likewise been involved with my errant husband, Brian), Robin Stokes, our unbelievably busy veterinary vicar, must be mightily relieved that his home can be fairly described as a compact, brick-built box. Des. det. res. 3 recs. 4 beds. c.h. with seemingly the only comforting addition being in the sturdy form of a two-oven Aga, Robin's reliable ally on which he leans for slow-cooked casseroles and country cakes.

SPICY LAMB

SERVES 2

If Robin keeps his sermon short, this should be perfectly timed for an instant lunch.

1lb (450g) lean lamb (without bone)
½ carton (2fl oz) plain yogurt
1tbsp curry powder
2 cloves garlic, crushed
2tbsp cooking oil
1 medium onion
20fl oz (600ml/1pt) stock (or use bouillon cube)
2 medium potatoes, diced
1oz (25g) sultanas
2oz (50g) long-grain rice
salt and freshly ground black pepper

Cut the lamb into bite-size pieces. Place the meat in a bowl with the yogurt, curry powder and crushed garlic. Mix well with a wooden spoon and leave to marinate for 2–3 hours.

When you are ready to cook the curry, heat the oil in a casserole and fry the onion until it is transparent. Add the stock and the diced lamb and its marinade and simmer while stirring and turning the meat. Add the potatoes, sultanas and rice. Sprinkle with salt and black pepper and bring to the boil.

Cover the casserole and cook in a moderate oven at 350°F/180°C/Gas 4 for 1–1½ hours.

COUNTRY · CUTTINGS

Caroline suggests making meringues with soft brown sugar, then they're deliciously caramel flavoured.

ROBIN'S BOBOTIE

SERVES 2

A savoury dish made with minced beef and almonds which Mrs Antrobus must have collected somewhere on her travels across Africa.

2 large onions, chopped
1tbsp cooking oil
1lb (450g) minced beef
1tbsp curry powder
1 slice bread, brown or white (crusts removed)
10fl oz (275ml/ ½pt) milk
1tbsp chopped almonds
juice of 1 lemon
1tsp dried mixed herbs
10fl oz (275ml/ ½pt) stock
salt and pepper
2 medium size eggs

Fry the chopped onion in the oil until transparent, then add the meat, stirring frequently until browned. Add the curry powder.

Soak the bread in a little of the milk, mash it with a fork and mix into the meat and onion. Add the chopped almonds, lemon juice, herbs, stock and seasoning. Cook the mixture slowly for a few minutes, then turn into an ovenproof dish. Beat the eggs with the remaining milk and pour it over the beef.

Cook in a slow to moderate oven at 325°F/160°C/Gas 3 for about an hour, until the top is brown and bubbling.

BRAISED OXTAIL WITH TURNIPS

SERVES 4

The delight of this recipe is that the longer it cooks the more delicious it becomes. Ideal for a busy vet eating his meals at odd times.

1 oxtail, cut into joints
2tbsp vegetable oil
2 onions, sliced
2 carrots, sliced
2 sticks celery, chopped
1lb (450g) young, small turnips
10fl oz (275ml/ ½pt) beef stock (or use a stock cube
5fl oz (150ml/ ¼pt) red wine
bouquet garni
salt and pepper

Trim the fat from the oxtail joints, rinse and dr
Heat the oil in a flameproof casserole, brow

the oxtail pieces and transfer to a plate.

Gently fry the onions, carrots, celery and whole, small turnips for about 2 minutes. Return the oxtail to the casserole placing the pieces on top of the vegetables. Add the stock, wine, bouquet garni and seasoning.

Cover the casserole, and either simmer on top of the stove for 2 hours or place in a low oven at 300°F/150°C/Gas 2 for 1½–2 hours until tender, the meat falling away from the bones.

Serve with a fluffy baked potato to soak up the rich gravy.

RHUBARB AND GINGER CRUMBLE

SERVES 4

Robin Stokes is an accomplished cake maker and his skill extends to pudding-making, too. Having discovered a clump of Richard Adamson's rhubarb fighting for survival in a corner of the vicarage garden, he decides to put it to good use. A jar of syrupy preserved ginger, given to Robin by an ardent parishioner, adds extra interest to this crumble's flavour.

2oz (50g) hard margarine or butter
4oz (100g) plain flour
2oz (50g) soft brown sugar
1tsp ground ginger
1lb (450g) rhubarb
1tbsp chopped preserved ginger
2tbsp ginger syrup
5oz (150g) caster sugar

Put the margarine into a bowl and rub into the flour until it resembles fine breadcrumbs. Stir in the soft brown sugar and ground ginger.

Peel the rhubarb sticks (unless they are very young and tender), and cut into ½in long pieces. Place these with the chopped preserved ginger and syrup and the caster sugar in a 2pt pie dish. Cover the fruit with the crumble mixture, pressing it down gently.

Bake in the oven at 350°F/180°C/Gas 4 for about 40 minutes until crisp and golden.

GREY GABLES COUNTRY CLUB

'COME ON IN BRIAN, but step on this newspaper with those muddy boots – can't you see I've just washed the floor?'

Spread on my kitchen's terracotta tiles, posing as a makeshift mat, was that telegraph of weekly news, The Borchester Echo. *Alongside Rodway & Watson's tempting details of country house sales, printed massively and boxed in bold black type, was the following advertisement:*

Grey Gables Country Club and Conference Centre

A privately owned *[by none other than the avuncular Jack Woolley of sound West Midland stock]* English country hotel with banqueting and conference facilities, Grey Gables Country Club lies halfway between Borchester and the historic cathedral city of Felpersham, in the heart of the Borsetshire countryside. Set in many acres *[only 15, let's be honest]* of immaculate *[depending entirely on Higgs' dyspeptic disposition]* gardens and parkland, this elegant *[what?]* Victorian Gothic mansion is the ideal setting for walking, shooting and fishing holidays and offers the fine facilities of its 18-hole golf course and club house.

This famous Country Club has 50 extensively *[not to mention expensively, according to my mother]* refurbished en suite bedrooms.

An à la carte menu is offered in our restaurant with excellent English and French cuisine by our experienced residential chef *[the infamous Jean Paul, renowned not only for his pâte sucrée, but for his frequent fits of French pique]*. Why not revel in a relaxing, rejuvenating weekend break in our Health Club? Swim in our heated indoor pool.

Enjoy the experience of our aromatherapy, sauna and jacuzzi. Partake of a light and healthy snack in the club's Health Food Express. Or maybe you prefer to wine, dine and dance *[not to Tommy Croker any more – please!]* on a Saturday night in this romantic retreat. For full details contact the manager Ms Caro . . .

And then I watched with glee as Brian's big green boot descended, blotting out that tantalising name . . . poor Caroline!

TERRINE D'AVOCATS ET D'ASPERGES

SERVES 4–6

This terrine of avocado and asparagus is a fresh, temptingly green starter. Jean Paul sprinkles each slice liberally with freshly picked and chopped herbs, and composes a sharp mustardy vinaigrette to serve with it. You could also try a spicy tomato sauce with the terrine.

12 plump asparagus spears
2 large avocados
juice of 1 lime
1oz (25g) gelatine
6fl oz (175ml) double cream
salt and freshly ground black pepper
Worcestershire or tabasco sauce, to taste (optional)

FOR THE VINAIGRETTE
4fl oz (100ml) olive oil
2tbsp white wine vinegar
½tsp caster sugar
2tsp Dijon mustard
salt and pepper

Trim the asparagus spears, discarding any tough, woody ends and knobbly lumps. Plunge into boiling salted water and cook gently until tender. Drain carefully.

Peel, stone and chop the avocados and put into a food processor or blender. Add the lime juice and purée until smooth, adding a little milk or cream if necessary.

In a basin, sprinkle the gelatine on to 3tbsp boiling water. Stir well and leave until dissolved.

In a saucepan, heat the cream until simmering – do not boil. Pour into the dissolved gelatine, stirring thoroughly, then sieve this creamy mixture into the avocado purée and season well, adding Worcestershire sauce or tabasco, if required.

Butter a 9in terrine, or loaf tin, and line with cling film or baking parchment. Spread a shallow layer of avocado mixture on the bottom of the terrine and arrange the asparagus spears on this. Season with salt and freshly ground black pepper and cover with the remaining avocado mixture. Cover with cling film and refrigerate for 24 hours.

To serve, stand the terrine in a sink of hot water to loosen. Turn the avocado loaf out on to a serving plate and garnish with fresh herbs. Cut slices with a sharp-bladed knife which has been dipped in hot water.

To make the vinaigrette, place all the ingredients in a screw-top jar and shake well. More mustard can be added to make it thicker.

COUNTRY · CUTTINGS

Mix together freshly chopped, boiled beetroot with soured cream and horseradish sauce – excellent with cold meats.

COQUILLES ST JACQUES AUX POIREAUX

SERVES 4

Delicately creamy and utterly delicious. For the fish course the scallops are served daintily in their shells.

12oz (350g) thin young leeks
2oz (50g) butter
8–12 scallops, shelled and cleaned
2 shallots, finely chopped
4fl oz (100ml) dry white wine
10fl oz (275ml/½pt) double cream
a pinch of cayenne
freshly ground nutmeg (optional)
salt and freshly ground black pepper

Cut off the green parts of the leeks and discard. Split the white parts in half, lengthways. Trim them and rinse thoroughly under the tap, then drain and cut into narrow strips 2in long.

Melt 1oz (25g) butter with 2fl oz (60ml) water in a heavy-based saucepan over a low heat. Add the leeks, cover and simmer for 15 minutes, stirring from time to time. When soft, remove from the heat and keep hot.

Rinse the scallops under cold, running water, removing any black threads. Cut the scallops in half horizontally.

Melt the remaining butter in a small pan, add the finely chopped shallots and cook until soft. Add the scallops with their corals and the white wine. Bring to the boil and simmer gently for 2–4 minutes, depending on the size of the scallops. (Do not overcook as the corals will be damaged and the white flesh toughened.) Remove the scallops and keep warm with the leeks.

Increase the heat to reduce the cooking juices from the scallops and the leeks to half, then add the cream. Bring to the boil briefly and season to taste, with salt and cayenne.

Serve the scallops on a bed of leeks. Pour over the cream sauce and sprinkle with nutmeg if required. Serve any extra sauce separately.

COUNTRY · CUTTINGS

Make a pincushion and stuff with sweet herbs – lavender, lemon verbena or rosemary – to scent your sewing basket.

Place a handful of lemon balm in the body cavity of a chicken before roasting.

SORBET À L'ORANGE

SERVES 6–8

A great appetite enhancer that's not too tart, not too sweet – and it doesn't taste like an ice lolly!

6 sugar lumps
orange peel
9fl oz (250g) still mineral water
3½oz (90g) icing sugar
9fl oz (250g) freshly squeezed orange juice
1tbsp lemon juice

Rub the orange peel with the lumps of sugar – the flavour will be absorbed into the sugar.

In a large bowl, put the mineral water, icing sugar and sugar lumps. Strain the freshly squeezed orange and lemon juice through a fine sieve and add to the mixture, stirring thoroughly. Transfer to an ice cream maker and freeze. If you don't possess an ice cream maker, place in a freezer container and freeze for 2–3 hours, or until almost solid.

Remove from the freezer and beat thoroughly to break down the ice crystals. Return to the freezer for 1–2 hours until completely set.

Serve the sorbet scooped out in balls.

MAGRETS DE CANARD AUX CERISES

SERVES 4

Sweet and rather rich, the duck breasts are presented attractively in a pool of cherry sauce. The light fluffy rice makes a happy marriage. It was just unfortunate that I happened to be eating this when Roger Travers-Macey appeared at Grey Gables.

4 large, boned duck breasts
3tbsp clear honey
1tbsp (175ml) lemon juice
6fl oz (175ml) dry white wine
1lb (450g) morello cherries or 15oz (425g) can pitted cherries in syrup
2tsp sugar
1½tsp arrowroot
4tbsp cherry brandy or port
salt and freshly ground black pepper

Score the skin of the duck breast with a sharp knife. Blend the honey and lemon juice and spread over the skins, then leave to marinade for 30 minutes. Place in a roasting tin, season and roast in the oven at 400°F/200°C/Gas 6 for about 30–40 minutes.

When cooked, take the duck breasts from the oven and transfer to a plate to keep warm. Skim any fat from the roasting pan, then place the pan over a high heat. Add the wine and stir with a wooden spoon to deglaze, reducing the liquid by half.

Remove the stones from the cherries, put the fruit to one side and add the cherry juice and sugar to the roasting pan, or the syrup from the canned cherries without extra sugar.

Blend the arrowroot with the cherry brandy or port and pour into the boiling pan, stirring until the sauce thickens. Add the cherries and cook gently for 2–3 minutes.

Slice the duck breasts and arrange in an attractive fan shape on the plate, pouring a little sauce over them. Serve the duck with wild rice and pine nuts.

WILD RICE AND PINE NUTS

SERVES 4

7oz (200g) long-grain rice
2oz (50g) wild rice
1tbsp butter
2tbsp sesame seed oil
2oz (50g) pine nut kernels
2 cloves garlic, chopped
salt and pepper

Cook the rice in boiling salted water until almost tender and then drain.

Melt the butter with the oil in a frying pan. Add the pine nut kernels and fry until golden, stir in the chopped garlic and heat through. Mix together with the rice and season to taste with salt and pepper.

ENDIVES BRAISÉES À L'ORANGE

SERVES 3–4

I'm not usually over-fond of this vegetable but the slightly bitter taste of chicory is cleverly masked when cooked this way with the delicious orangey butter.

6 large endives (chicory)
3tbsp butter
2tsp sugar
juice and rind of 1 orange
salt and black pepper

Trim and rinse the endives, discarding any bruised outer leaves.

Melt the butter in a heavy-bottomed ovenproof casserole. Arrange the endives in the dish, laying thin strips of orange peel between them. Sprinkle with sugar and orange juice and season lightly with salt and pepper.

Cover with a tightly fitting lid and bake in a moderately hot oven 350°F/180°C/Gas 4 for about 30–40 minutes or until the endives feel soft when pierced with a sharp knife. Remove the orange peel and serve hot.

TARTE AU CITRON

SERVES 6

I get the feeling that this is a slightly simplified version of most of Jean Paul's delicate pastry concoctions. Do use unwaxed fruit, and if you prefer the tart sharper to the taste buds, use more lemon zest.

4oz (100g) butter
6oz (175g) plain flour
1oz (25g) icing sugar
1tbsp water

FOR THE FILLING
4oz (100g) caster sugar
3 medium size eggs, separated
grated rind and juice of 1 orange and 1 large lemon
5fl oz (150ml/¼pt) double cream
1oz (25g) icing sugar

In a saucepan melt the butter over a low heat and sieve in the flour and icing sugar, add the water and mix to a soft dough.

Press into an 8in flan tin or dish, prick the base with a fork and bake blind for 15 minutes at 350°F/180°C/Gas 4.

To make the filling, put the caster sugar, egg yolks and grated rind in a bowl. Whisk thoroughly. Beat in the cream and juice until blended.

Beat the egg whites until stiff and carefully fold into the mixture. Pour into the cooked pastry case.

Lower the oven temperature to 300°F/150°C/Gas 2 and cook until golden brown and set.

Sieve icing sugar over the tart before serving with whipped cream, fromage frais or yogurt.

MOUSSE AU CASSIS

SERVES 4–6

Jean Paul serves each little mousse turned out into a pool of blackcurrant coulis.

12oz (350g) fresh blackcurrants
apple mint leaves
4oz (100g) caster sugar
6 medium size egg yolks
7fl oz (200ml) double cream
3 medium size egg whites

Remove the stalks from the blackcurrants, place in a saucepan with a few mint leaves and about 4tbsp water and cook until soft. Purée in a blender or liquidiser and pass through a sieve.

Put the purée, sugar and egg yolks in a large bowl over a pan of boiling water. Whisk until thick, then remove from the heat and continue to whisk until cool.

Whip the cream lightly and fold into the blackcurrant mixture.

Whisk the egg whites until they are stiff but not dry, and with a slotted spoon fold into the creamy mixture. Pour into individual dishes and chill in the refrigerator for 3–4 hours. Decorate each with a small mint leaf.

☆ GREY GABLES HEALTH CLUB ☆

There's an enticing assortment of herb teas served in the Health Club – not just the packeted varieties with the bags dangling on strings, but those made from fresh herbs, found in scented abundance in Jean Paul's herb garden.
Caroline suggests fresh, clear, startlingly green peppermint tea as a lightning 'pick-me-up', or lemon balm as a relaxing drink, ideal for evenings. Lovage, enhanced with a grinding of sea salt, will make a celery-flavoured beverage and of course camomile, the age-old favourite, is wonderful for settling the tummy. Infuse the flowers only briefly to enjoy its delicate flavour.

AUTUMN SALAD WITH MUSTARD DRESSING

SERVES 4–6

This does look desperately dull but is enlivened visually by the bright green watercress. The flavour, however, is wholesome and reassuringly healthy.

1lb (450g) potatoes (Pink Fir Apple or Jersey Royals are ideal)
2 celery hearts
8oz (225g) fresh chestnuts
a bunch of watercress
1 large clove garlic, halved
8oz (225g) cold, lean cooked chicken, diced
2tbsp balsamic vinegar
salt and black pepper

FOR THE DRESSING
4fl oz (100ml) fromage frais or Pat Archer's low fat plain yogurt
1tbsp Dijon mustard
1tbsp wine vinegar

Steam the potatoes until cooked but not too soft and then cut into quarters.

Rinse and chop the celery hearts. Peel the chestnuts, remove the brown furry skins, and chop. Rinse the watercress and remove any long tough stalks. Rub a salad bowl with the cut garlic.

Toss the warm potatoes with the chicken, chestnuts and celery. Add the balsamic vinegar and seasoning.

To make the dressing, mix all the ingredients together and pour over the salad. Serve decorated with watercress.

CHILLED SUMMER SOUP

SERVES 3–4

Personally, I prefer soups that in the last resort can be served hot or cold. You have to be absolutely certain that the evening will be fine and warm if you intend serving this at a dinner party.

1 cucumber, peeled and chopped
1 small onion, chopped
4oz (100g) prawns, chopped
12fl oz (350g) natural low fat yogurt
1 or 2 drops tabasco sauce
10fl oz (275g/½pt) chicken stock
2tbsp finely chopped chives, mint and parsley
salt and pepper

Place the cucumber and onion in a food processor or blender and blend until smooth. Add the prawns, yogurt and tabasco and blend again. Pour into a large bowl and stir in the cooled stock and chopped herbs, and season to taste. Add more yogurt if needed.

Serve chilled in a bowl with ice cubes.

Rosy Tomato and Lentil Soup

SERVES 6

This is so very quick and simple to make, with no oil to make it fattening. Perhaps you could allow yourself a warm, crusty wholemeal roll – without butter of course – or a sprinkling of croûtons.

2 large tins (14oz/400g) plum tomatoes
3 red onions, chopped
6oz (175g) red lentils
1tsp tomato purée
bouquet garni
40fl oz (1.2L/2pt) vegetable stock (made with a stock cube)
salt and freshly ground black pepper

Simmer the tinned tomatoes with the vegetables, tomato purée and bouquet garni in 900ml (1½pt) stock until the vegetables are tender. Remove the bouquet garni and purée the soup in a blender or food processor. Add the remaining stock, and season to taste.

Lime Rhubarb Refresher

SERVES 3–4

Much more attractive when young, pink, forced rhubarb is used – it's sweeter too and has a much more delicate flavour.

1lb (450g) rhubarb, trimmed and cut into 1in lengths, or a 1lb 3oz (539g) can, drained
5fl oz (150ml/¼pt) lime cordial
2tbsp honey, or to taste
juice and peel of 1 small lime
½oz (15g) gelatine

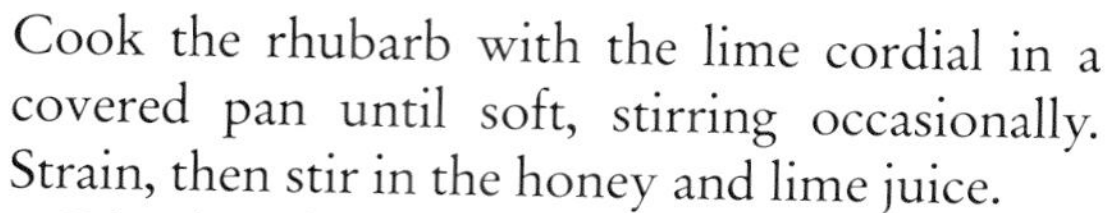

Cook the rhubarb with the lime cordial in a covered pan until soft, stirring occasionally. Strain, then stir in the honey and lime juice.

Dissolve the gelatine in 2tbsp boiling water and stir into the cooked rhubarb. Pour into individual glasses and chill until set.

Serve with yogurt and a twist of lime peel to decorate.

Lemon Cheese Whip

SERVES 6

If you can allow yourself a few more calories, mix 6oz (175g) digestive biscuit crumbs into 3oz (75g) melted butter and line a 7in loose-bottomed cake tin with the mixture. Pour in the filling and, hey presto, you have a simple cheesecake that everyone can enjoy.

1 lemon jelly
6fl oz (175ml) hot water
1tbsp clear honey
grated rind and juice of 2 small lemons
8oz (225g) low fat curd cheese
6oz can (170g) evaporated milk, chilled

Dissolve the jelly in the hot water, add the honey and squeeze in the lemon juice. Leave until cool.

In a blender, cream together the curd cheese and lemon rind and add the almost-set jelly.

Whisk the chilled evaporated milk and fold into the cheese mixture.

Pour into individual dishes and leave to set in the refrigerator.

OVER-SIXTIES' CHRISTMAS PARTY

St Stephens's Church clock wheezes, pauses, then strikes seven times. A low mist hovers over the Am. Smoke hangs atop chimney stacks on crouching cottages. This is December, dank and dreary.

The cheery mainstays of Manorfield Close bear down on the village hall in greedy anticipation.

'Well, you tell me, Jean Harvey, where you can get a slap-up three-course meal for £3.50 then? Them fish 'n chips at Weston on the trip was more than that – and 'alf of them was cold . . . and Loxley Barratt's lot get the bus thrown in.'

The glossy doors swing open and a wall of warmth greets them, along with the clattering of crockery and conversation. Rubber heels and ferrules squeak on waxed wooden floorboards, while Marjorie Antrobus's remarkably unrheumatic fingers give a jaunty rendition of Rudolf the Red-Nosed Reindeer. Stout trestles and indescribable undergarments creak as ample bosoms and bottoms ease themselves into place. A curious haze of camphor and wintergreen wafts around Joe and his Sunday-best corduroys. Steaming willow-patterned cups of tea are eagerly passed along the rows. There's a snapping of crackers and cracking of jokes and rather vulgar paper hats gluing themselves to glistening foreheads. Sid Perks struggles manfully into the moth-eaten garb of a steadily suffocating Father Christmas.

That's right – you've guessed, it's none other than The Ambridge and District Over-Sixties Annual Christmas Party!

UNCLE WALTER'S PICKLED WALNUTS IN SPICED VINEGAR

Old Walter Gabriel used to collect the nuts and Mrs Perkins, with much grumbling, pickled them for him. He enjoyed them with a thick succulent slice of cold ham.

If you are lucky enough to have access to a walnut tree, pick the walnuts in June or July when they are young and green, before their shells have formed. Prick them all over with a large bodkin and put them in a dish covered with brine (6oz (175g) salt to 60fl oz/1.7L/3pt water).

Drain them after 3 days and spread them on a tray in the daylight until they have turned black. When completely black put into wide-necked jars and cover with cold spiced vinegar (2lb walnuts to 2pt vinegar), then seal with air-tight, vinegar-proof tops and label.

FOR THE SPICED VINEGAR
40fl oz (1.2L/2pt) malt vinegar
½oz (15g) cloves
½oz (15g) black peppercorns
½oz (15g) whole allspice
1oz (25g) mustard seeds

Bring all the ingredients to the boil, then remove from heat and leave to cool. Stand for 2–3 hours then strain through muslin. If any of the vinegar is to be kept, make sure you use bottles with corks or vinegar-proof lids.

COUNTRY · CUTTINGS

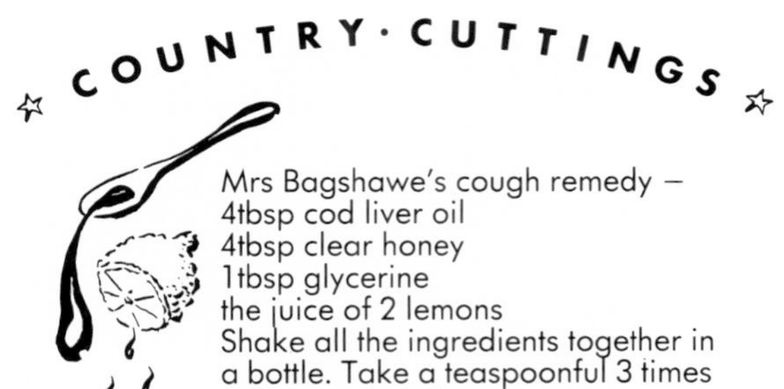

Mrs Bagshawe's cough remedy –
4tbsp cod liver oil
4tbsp clear honey
1tbsp glycerine
the juice of 2 lemons
Shake all the ingredients together in a bottle. Take a teaspoonful 3 times a day in a little hot water.

MUSTARD CRUSTED HAM

SERVES 8–10

This is perfect for a party if you're feeding a lot of people. Serve with Sweet Pickled Cinnamon Pears (see p69).

2½–3lb (1.125–1.4kg) gammon or collar
2tbsp clear honey
2tbsp wine vinegar
2tbsp demerara sugar
2tbsp coarse-grain mustard

Soak the bacon in a saucepan of cold water overnight to remove salt, changing the water to cook. Weigh the joint to calculate the cooking time, allowing 25 minutes per lb (450g) plus 25 minutes. Cover and simmer for half the required cooking time. Remove the bacon from the liquid. Wrap in foil and place in a roasting tin. Bake in the oven at 350°F/180°C/Gas 4 until 30 minutes before the cooking time is complete.

Remove the foil, cut off the rind and score the fatty surface of the joint. Heat the honey and vinegar together and pour over the joint. Mix the sugar and mustard together and press into the surface of the ham where the rind has been removed.

Return to the oven at an increased temperature of 400°F/200°C/Gas 6 to finish cooking.

When cold, slice as thinly as possible.

WINTER SALAD WITH YOGURT DRESSING

SERVES 8–10 AS A SIDE SALAD

This crisp salad with its smooth dressing makes a fine accompaniment to roast ham, hot from the oven with a honey and mustard crusted coating.

FOR THE SALAD
1 small white cabbage, finely shredded
½ head celery, trimmed and sliced
4oz (100g) chopped walnut pieces
2 leeks, the white part cleaned and finely sliced
8oz (225g) carrots, grated

FOR THE YOGURT DRESSING
5oz (150g) natural yogurt
1tbsp olive oil
2tsp cider, wine vinegar or lemon juice
1tsp wholegrain or Dijon mustard
salt and pepper

To make the salad, combine all the ingredients.

To make the dressing, mix all the ingredients together thoroughly. Add chopped parsley or chives if preferred, and season to taste. Pour this dressing over the salad.

GINGER TIPSY TRIFLE

SERVES 8–10

This should *serve 10 people, or 8 greedy ones!*

FOR THE BASE
1 fatless ginger sponge (or a packet of fatless sponge cakes)
1lb (450g) ginger marmalade
¼ bottle ginger wine (approximately 2 wineglasses)
20fl oz (600ml/1pt) home-made Rich Custard Cream or a packet variety

FOR THE TOPPING
20fl oz (600ml/1pt) double cream
2oz (50g) split blanched almonds
2oz (50g) crystallized ginger

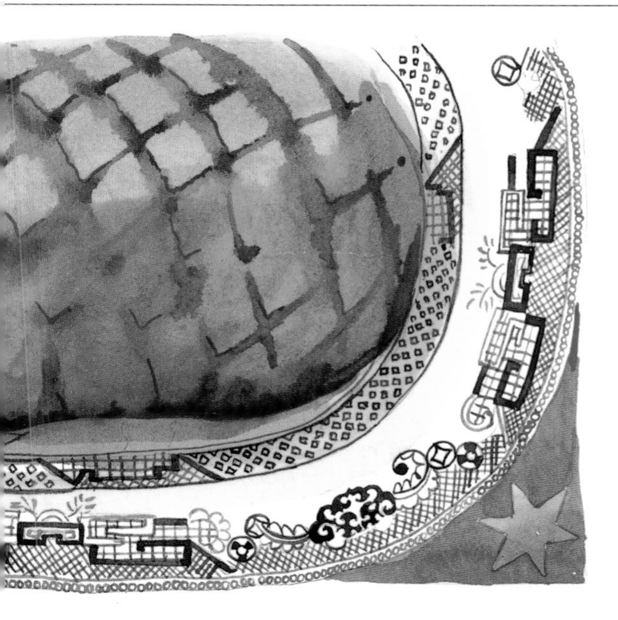

For the fatless ginger sponge, follow the same recipe as the Chocolate Yuletide Log, substituting 1tsp ground ginger for the chocolate.

Bake either in two 7in sponge cake tins or in a Swiss roll tin. Cool flat on a wire tray and cut into 1in fingers.

Split the sponge cake fingers and sandwich with the ginger marmalade. Place at the bottom of a glass bowl. Pour the ginger wine over the sponge and cover with a layer of the custard, then chill.

To make the topping, whip the cream until it stands in peaks and spread a thick layer over the custard. Decorate with split, blanched almonds and crystallized ginger.

RICH CUSTARD CREAM

2tbsp caster sugar
20fl oz (600ml/1pt) milk
½ vanilla pod
4 medium size eggs

Put the sugar, milk and vanilla pod in a saucepan and slowly bring to the boil. Remove the vanilla pod and pour the milk over the beaten eggs, whisking briskly.

Return the sauce to the pan and continue to cook over a low heat, stirring until the sauce thickens. Do not allow it to boil otherwise it will curdle.

CHOCOLATE YULETIDE LOG

SERVES 6–8

Some grumble that this is not a conventional Christmas cake, but there's no fear of raisin seeds finding their way under Mrs Potter's dentures with this deliciously rich recipe!

3 large size eggs
4oz (100g) caster sugar
3oz (75g) plain flour
1oz (25g) cocoa
1tbsp hot water

FOR THE CHOCOLATE BUTTER CREAM
4oz (100g) butter
8oz (225g) icing sugar
4oz (100g) plain dark chocolate (melted)
2tbsp strong black coffee

Grease and line a 12 × 9in Swiss roll tin.

Whisk the eggs and sugar in a bowl with an electric hand whisk, over a pan of hot water, until pale and creamy. Sift in the flour and cocoa, folding in with a metal spoon. Gently stir in the hot water.

Pour into the prepared tin and bake in a preheated oven at 400°F/200°C/Gas 6 for approximately 10 minutes, or until the cake feels springy when lightly pressed.

Turn the cake out on to greaseproof paper and roll it up with a layer of well-sugared greaseproof paper inside. Allow to cool.

To make the chocolate butter cream, beat the softened butter with the sifted icing sugar until fluffy, then thoroughly stir in the melted chocolate and coffee.

When the cake is cold, gently remove the paper and spread the cake with a little of the chocolate butter cream. Reroll it and decorate with the remaining cream, using a fork to make the tree bark markings. Dust with icing sugar and decorate with a Christmas robin.

GRANGE FARM

YOUNG EDWARD GRUNDY, his worn woollen elbows leaning on the crumpled tablecloth, gulps the last juicy mouthful of Clarrie's damson pie, pushing the eighth smooth, round, pebble-like stone to the rim of his pudding plate. 'Tinker, tailor, soldier, sailor . . .'

No time to waste, he scrapes back his chair across the lumpy linoed floor and races out into the pot-holed yard. Chickens and kittens scatter as he and William skid out through the leaning five-barred gate, racing each other on their mudguard-rattling, rusting bikes.

On sunlit days of early spring they see snow-white blackthorn blossom and catkin-tasselled coppices, where the silence is broken only by chattering blackbirds or the joking laugh of a green woodpecker. They know where to collect the jewelled strings of toadspawn from damp ditches with celandine covered banks. On warm June days they see bramble-tangled hedgerows busy with the murmuring drone of bees, and filled with cream-lace elderflowers and shell-pink dog roses. In late summer they try to catch the tawny tortoiseshells as they flit from sun-brindled hawthorn berries to bristling teasel and field thistle. This is the true richness of the Ambridge countryside.

But the Grundy home is a poor and run-down place. Its shoddily rendered brick walls are cracked and crumbling, window frames are rotting and roof tiles slip into rickety unfixed guttering. The bi-annually due rent is grudgingly paid on Michaelmas and Lady Day with poverty-line profits.

Inside Grange Farm curmudgeonly Joe sits slumped in his

cushion-sagging chair, wheezing and supposedly dozing. A strong smell of home-made embrocation permeates the kitchen. Rows of holey woollen socks and dripping interlock vests droop and steam over the solid-fuel stove. Hot and care-worn Clarrie sweeps and mops, waging a war against dirt and grime, desperate to escape to the relative relaxation of The Bull. *But the boorish old beggar grunts, stretches and grumbles back into life, gasping for her to brew him a mug of strong, sweet tea.*

Meanwhile, craftily thieving horn-hatted Eddie, ferret in pocket and sack in hand, moves stealthily down the shadowy edge of Brian's game-rich coverts. Rabbits scuttle back to their warrens and burrows. Pheasants rustle in the hedgerow thickets, making their wintry evening throaty chuckle. A lone barn owl hoots eerily in the twilit distance. Eddie licks his smiling lips, thinks succulent supper-time thoughts, smells the savoury stews, tastes the richly gravied roasts, then follows this feast with damson pie . . .

'Rich man, poor man, beggar man, thief.'

LIZZIE LARKIN'S COUNTRY LOAF

This recipe, which should be enough for two loaves, is quick and simple to make and requires no yeast. It freezes well too.

8oz (225g) wholewheat flour
8oz (225g) plain flour
2tsp cream of tartar
1tsp (level) salt
1tsp bicarbonate of soda
1tsp sugar
2oz (50g) margarine or lard
10fl oz (275ml/½pt) sour milk or buttermilk

Grease and flour a baking tray. Sift the dry ingredients twice. Rub in the lard and mix to a loose dough with the milk, adding a little at a time. Knead the dough lightly on a surface sprinkled with brown flour.

Shape into two loaves, leave for 10 minutes and then bake at 375°F/190°C/Gas 5 for 30 minutes. Eat while very fresh.

FRUIT AND NUT PAN SCONES

MAKES 8

This is William and Edward's special tea-time treat. Foraging in the soft earth under the hazel trees in the hedgerows, the boys fill their pockets with nuts on autumn afternoons. Keep them until winter for a better flavour.

8oz (225g) wholemeal flour (plain)
½tsp bicarbonate of soda
1tsp cream of tartar
2oz (50g) margarine
1oz (25g) soft brown sugar
1oz (25g) chopped dates
1oz (25g) chopped hazelnuts
milk to mix

Sift the flour, bicarbonate of soda and cream of tartar together. Rub in the margarine until the mixture resembles fine breadcrumbs. Add the sugar, chopped dates and nuts and mix with a little milk.

Lightly grease a large frying pan and warm on a low hotplate.

Knead the dough into a round and roll out to fit the pan. Cut across into eight segments, and then put into the pan and cover with a lid.

Cook on a medium heat for about 5 minutes. When well risen turn over and cook on the other side for a further 5 minutes.

The scones are ready when they sound hollow when tapped on the bottom. Put on a wire tray to cool, between the folds of a clean tea towel – and to keep away thieving fingers! Spread with butter.

ROSIE'S ROCK BUNS

MAKES ABOUT 12

Clarrie's sister Rosie suggested this simple recipe.

8oz (225g) plain flour
½tsp salt
2tsp baking powder
2oz (50g) margarine or butter
1oz (25g) lard
3oz (75g) brown sugar
2oz (50g) currants
2oz (50g) candied peel
½tsp cinnamon
1 medium size egg
a little milk
a little extra sugar and cinnamon

Sift the flour, salt and baking powder into a bowl. Rub in the butter and fat. When it resembles fine breadcrumbs add the sugar, currants, peel and cinnamon.

Beat the egg with a little milk, make a well in the centre of the dry ingredients and pour this in, mixing thoroughly.

Place the mixture in little rounds on a greased baking tray and sprinkle the tops with the remaining sugar and cinnamon.

Bake for about 15 minutes at 450°F/230°C/Gas 8.

COUNTRY · CUTTINGS

Mabel Larkin used to boil her new rope clothes line in the copper before using it, to prevent it from stretching and to make it last longer.

FAMOUS FRUIT CAKE

Everyone in Ambridge seems to know about Clarrie's fruit cake. Jethro used to take a good hefty slice of this for his 'elevenses' when he worked up at Brookfield.

4oz (100g) margarine or butter
5fl oz (150ml/¼pt) water
1lb (450g) mixed fruit (currants, sultanas and peel)
1tbsp chunky marmalade
2 medium size eggs
8oz (225g) plain flour
1tsp mixed spice
8oz (225g) soft brown sugar
½tsp bicarbonate of soda
1tsp vinegar

Melt the butter in a saucepan and add the water and mixed fruit. Bring to the boil and simmer for 5 minutes, then allow to cool.

Add the marmalade, beaten eggs, sifted flour and spice and sugar. Mix well and add the bicarbonate of soda dissolved in the vinegar.

Grease and line an 8in cake tin and bake the mixture in this for approximately 1½ hours at 350°F/180°C/Gas 4. Test with a skewer.

AUTUMN SOUP

SERVES 6

Early on October mornings, with the mist floating over the fields, the plump mushrooms appear like magic in the dew-logged grass where horses have grazed in ages past – a beggar's harvest! If Joe doesn't eat them all for breakfast, Clarrie cooks this wholesome soup.

3oz (75g) butter
1 medium onion, finely chopped
1lb (450g) field mushrooms
1tbsp (heaped) plain flour
3oz (75g) chopped walnuts
20fl oz (600ml/1pt) milk
20fl oz (600ml/1pt) chicken stock (or stock cube)
½tsp salt
pepper
4fl oz (100ml) single cream

Melt the butter in a large saucepan and soften the onion until transparent. Add the washed and chopped mushrooms and fry gently for 2–3 minutes. Stir in the flour and walnuts and slowly add the milk and stock. Bring to the boil and simmer for half an hour.

Pour back into the saucepan and season with salt and pepper. Heat before serving, adding a swirl of cream to each bowlful if you're feeling generous! Cool a little before liquidising if a smoother soup is preferred.

NOTE Take extreme care if collecting mushrooms from the wild. Do not eat any mushroom unless you are *absolutely sure* you have identified it as edible.

COUNTRY · CUTTINGS

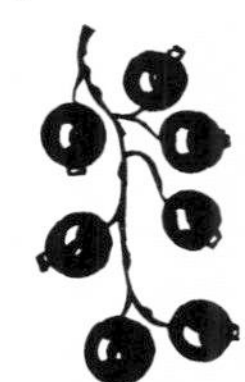

'Instead of sloe gin why not try blackcurrant gin?' says Clarrie. To a litre of gin add 1lb (450g) bruised, clean blackcurrants and 1lb (450g) demerara sugar. Soak in a stone jar for 3 months, stirring occasionally. Strain through a muslin cloth and bottle. Hide from Joe and Eddie!

LEEK AND TURNIP BOULANGÈRE

SERVES 4–6

Scattered with breadcrumbs and grated cheese, this could be a meal on its own.

1lb (450g) leeks
2lb (1kg) turnips
black pepper and salt
5fl oz (150ml/¼pt) chicken or vegetable stock
5fl oz (150ml/¼pt) milk
2oz (50g) margarine or butter
freshly grated nutmeg

Wash the leeks very thoroughly, removing all the grit, then chop thinly.

Peel the turnips and slice finely.

Grease a wide, shallow baking dish and place a layer of turnip on the bottom, followed by a layer of leeks and seasoning. Continue to arrange the vegetables in layers.

Pour the stock and milk over, dotting the final layer of turnip with margarine or butter, and then sprinkling with freshly ground nutmeg.

Bake in the oven for 45 minutes at 350°F/180°C/Gas 4.

HARVESTER'S RABBIT WITH SAGE DUMPLINGS

SERVES 4–6

A different recipe from the ordinary rabbit casserole, but Joe isn't keen on the 'fancy' orange slices. Clarrie insists next time she'll put in some chopped streaky bacon instead. 'Anything for a quiet life!'

1 skinned rabbit, cut into 6 portions
a little flour
oil or butter for frying
2 onions, sliced
10fl oz (275ml/½pt) brown ale
1 orange, scrubbed and thinly sliced
1tsp mixed herbs
salt and black pepper

FOR THE DUMPLINGS
4oz (100g) self-raising flour
2oz (50g) shredded suet
1tbsp freshly snipped sage
1tbsp freshly snipped chives
salt and pepper
water to mix

Wash the rabbit portions, dry and toss in seasoned flour. Heat the oil in a pan and fry the rabbit for a few minutes until brown, then transfer the joints to a casserole.

Fry the sliced onions until transparent, then put with the rabbit.

Stir the ale into the residue in the pan and add the orange, herbs and seasoning. Reduce the liquid a little by boiling, then pour into the casserole.

Cover the casserole and cook in a moderate oven at 350°F/180°C/Gas 4 for 1½ hours.

Meanwhile prepare the dumplings by mixing the flour, suet, herbs and seasoning thoroughly. Then add just enough water to make a firm dough. Turn on to a floured board, cut into pieces and roll into balls. Drop these into the casserole 15 minutes before the rabbit is cooked, replacing the lid.

Place sprigs of bitter-smelling rue on larder shelves to deter ants.

PENNY-WISE PIE

SERVES 4–6

Clarrie says she can usually find the ingredients for this filling pie in the larder – sometimes she adds some snipped pieces of bacon too. It makes a good, nourishing meal that costs very little.

FOR THE PASTRY
6oz (175g) plain wholemeal flour
2oz (50g) plain white flour
pinch salt
2oz (50g) butter or hard margarine
2oz (50g) lard
2tbsp cold water

FOR THE FILLING
12oz (350g) potatoes
2 large onions
3tbsp vegetable oil
4oz (100g) mature, grated cheddar cheese
2tbsp single cream or milk
1tbsp chopped parsley and chives
salt and pepper

Mix flours and salt in a bowl. Cut the fats into small pieces, then rub between the fingers until the mixture resembles fine breadcrumbs. Add the water and stir with a knife until the mixture gathers into a ball. Turn on to a floured board and knead slightly.

Grease a 9in pie dish or flan tin. Roll out the pastry and line the dish.

To make the filling, boil the potatoes until tender. Chop the onions and sauté in the oil until soft. Mix the onions and potatoes together and add grated cheddar cheese, cream, chopped parsley and chives and salt and pepper to taste.

Allow to cool, then fill the pastry case and dot with butter. Brush the edges of the pastry with water. Cover with a pastry lid and seal. Decorate with pastry leaves and prick the lid with a fork.

Bake in the centre of a hot oven at 425°F/220°C/Gas 7 for about 30 minutes until cooked through.

FRENCH APPLE TART

SERVES 6

Bursting with enthusiasm after her visit to France, Clarrie was encouraged by Jean Paul to try some simple French recipes. Here's one that she favours for high days and holidays.

FOR THE PÂTE SUCRÉE
8oz (225g) plain flour
salt
6oz (175g) butter or margarine
1oz (25g) icing sugar
1 medium size egg yolk
1tbsp cold water

FOR THE FILLING
2lb (1kg) cooking apples
a little butter
4oz (100g) caster sugar
grated rind of 1 orange
grated rind of ½ lemon

To make the pâte sucrée, sift the flour and salt together and mix in the butter, icing sugar and yolk of egg with your fingertips, adding water if necessary. Knead the pastry until smooth. Then wrap in polythene and chill for half an hour.

To make the filling, core the apples and slice, unpeeled, into a buttered pan. Cover and cook over a gentle heat until soft. Pass the apples through a sieve, adding the sugar and orange and lemon zest to the purée. Cook again until the purée thickens, then allow to cool.

Roll the pastry out thinly to line a 9in flan tin, then bake blind at 400°F/200°C/Gas 6 for about 15 minutes, or until the pastry is set.

When cool, pile the cold apple mixture into the flan case and serve with whipped cream or yogurt.

COUNTRY·CUTTINGS

Lizzie Larkin used to polish her black kitchen range with black boot polish, black lead and turpentine. Brushed on and then polished off, this kept the range brilliant for a month.

JOE'S HOME-MADE CIDER

'Bending doesn't 'arf get my back.' Nevertheless Joe soon manages to gather up enough windfalls from the orchard to make this sparkling brew, which should be clear and ready to drink in three months – if he can keep away from it that long! Add a slice of beetroot if you like – it does improve the colour. Joe insists this is his genuine recipe.

Pick up all the windfall apples you can find, the smaller the better. A mixture of cookers and dessert apples is ideal. No need to peel or core them, just cut them up in chunks and put in an earthenware bowl covered in Grange Farm spring water! Add a lemon cut in quarters and a small piece of root ginger.

Leave for 2 weeks or so covered with a clean cloth, stirring once a day.

Strain, and then add 8oz (225g) sugar for every pint of liquid. Stir each day for 4 days, then bottle in good, strong bottles.

SPICED HEDGEROW JELLY

On a mellow September afternoon, the bees humming dozily and drunkenly on the ripe fruit, Clarrie finds it peaceful and relaxing to pick berries for her jam-making.

This jelly is good in puddings or with cold meat.

3lb (1.4kg) blackberries
3lb (1.4kg) elderberries
1tsp cloves tied in muslin
2 lemons
20fl oz (600ml/1pt) water
sugar (see below for quantity)

Pick over and clean up the blackberries, and strip the elderberries from their stalks and wash them. Put the fruit in the preserving pan with the cloves. Add the juice of the 2 lemons and water. Bring slowly to the boil and boil for 45 minutes, bruising the fruit with a wooden spoon until all the juice has run out. Then remove the bag of cloves and strain the fruit through a muslin cloth or jelly bag.

Measure the juice and weigh out the sugar, allowing 12oz (350g) for each pint of juice.

Return the juice to the clean pan and boil for 15 minutes. Add the warmed sugar, stir until it dissolves and then bring to the boil. Boil fast for about 10 minutes, or until the jelly sets.

COUNTRY · CUTTINGS

Joe's cure for farmers' lung – Mix together the juice of a freshly squeezed lemon with 1tbsp of clear honey, 1tbsp glycerine and 2tbsp whisky. Take sips until the wheezing and coughing subsides, topping up with whisky as required.

The Larkins family laxative – Mince finely together 2oz (50g) prunes, 2oz (50g) stoned dates, 2oz (50g) figs and 2oz (50g) seedless raisins with 1oz (25g) senna leaves. Keep in a screw-top jar. Dose: ½–1tsp when needed.

BETTY TUCKER'S BUDGET BAKE

Betty Tucker handed this recipe on to Clarrie, telling her how easy and economical it is. This should be enough for 4 or 5 portions. Her advice is to shrink or stretch the ingredients according to what you find in the larder.

1lb (450g) potatoes
2tbsp vegetable oil
½ small firm white cabbage, shredded
8oz (225g) streaky bacon, cut into strips
4oz (100g) mushrooms, sliced
salt and pepper
1 large tin (400g) of tomatoes, including the juice
1tsp dried herbs
8oz (225g) grated cheddar cheese

Parboil the potatoes, drain and cut into slices.

Heat the oil in a pan and quickly fry the cabbage, bacon and mushrooms until soft, but not brown. Pile into an ovenproof casserole with the chopped potatoes, seasoning and tomatoes and their juice. (Make the tomato juice up to 10fl oz (275ml/½pt) if necessary.) Sprinkle with herbs and top with grated cheese.

Bake at 350°F/180°C/Gas 4 for 1–1½ hours until browned on top and cooked through.

BAGGY'S BEAN BAKE

SERVES 3–4

Eddie has named this dish after his dubious friend Baggy. Much to Clarrie's annoyance they simply used all her tins of baked beans.

1lb (450g) haricot beans
8oz (225g) belly of pork
2 medium onions
2tsp salt
1tsp dry mustard
1tbsp brown sugar
2tbsp molasses or treacle
2tbsp vinegar
pinch of ground cinnamon
pinch of ground cloves
½tsp Worcestershire sauce

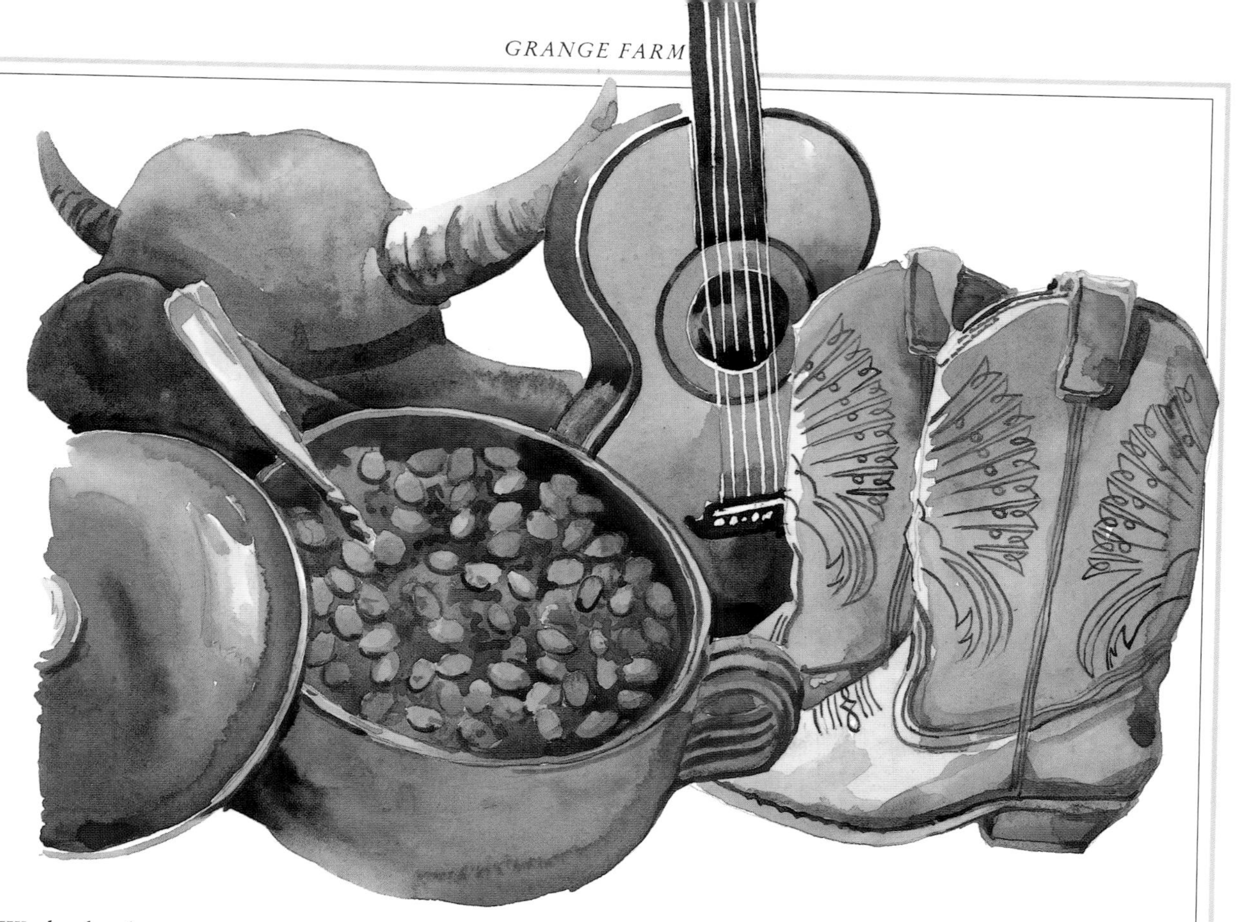

Wash the beans, cover with cold water and leave to soak overnight. Drain, cover with fresh water and cook slowly until tender.

Cut the pork into cubes. Then peel and slice the onions and put these with the beans and pork into a large casserole. Add enough water to cover and then stir in all the remaining ingredients.

Cover with a close-fitting lid and bake in a slow oven at 300°F/150°C/Gas 2 for 6–8 hours.

EDDIE'S SAUCY SPARE RIBS

A Country and Western evening at Grange Farm, the smoky smell of the barbecue on the evening air, the sound of Eddie's warbling tones as he entertains the punters, resplendent in his checked shirt and cow-horn hat, and the feel of crisp bank notes passing through Joe's fingers as he sits at the ricketty five-barred gate.

There's never that much meat on spare ribs, so it's best not to separate them but barbecue the whole rack.

2tbsp cooking oil
1 large onion, finely chopped
4oz (100g) tomato purée
4tbsp vinegar
3tbsp soft brown sugar
4tbsp Worcestershire sauce
2tsp dry mustard
salt and pepper
rack of spare ribs

Heat the oil in a saucepan, add the onion and fry for 3 minutes, stirring until the onion is transparent, but not brown. Stir in the tomato purée, then add the remaining ingredients and simmer the sauce over a low heat for 10 minutes, stirring frequently. Thin with a little water if necessary.

Rub salt into the ribs and cook for more than an hour over a low fire, turning and brushing with the sauce until brown.

HARVEST SUPPER

'COME, YE THANKFUL PEOPLE, COME' . . . to the annual harvest supper in the village hall, the third week of pheasant-shooting, nut-picking, leaf-dropping October.

No longer poised in pointed stooks in ochre-stubbled fields, the golden-yellow sheaves are now entwined with old man's beard and burnished beech mast, leaning against the platform. On the window ledge the russet Ribston pippins, mottled and plump, are perched with other fruits picked specially from Ambridge orchards. Bronze chrysanthemums, eternally autumnal, are interspersed with crusty, corn-shaped cottage loaves along the laden linen-covered tables.

'All is safely gather'd in' . . . and garnered into the safety of great grain storage silos. The costly combine, cosseted and covered, is stowed away until another summer. The electric blowers have blown their best, the winds of change have blown their worst. Or have they? Blossom and Boxer no longer plod their heavy shaggy hooves along the Borset clay to earn their keep. But acres of fields, of weeds and wind-blown flowers, are set aside for set-aside and subsidies – and hay?

The fresh-faced Ambridge farming folk sit amicably together, and fraternally side-by-side, Brian rubbing tweeded shoulders with the worn and worsted ones of weary Tony. They raise their effervescent glasses to thirsty lips, clear their dusty throats and praise the Lord, and the PCC, for 'Harvest-home'.

SPICY SEPTEMBER CHUTNEY

A perennial favourite which Gran Archer used to make years ago – and so did Auntie Pru. 'Always use sound, ripe fruit gathered on a dry day' . . . it says, written in a faint sloping hand.

3lb (1.4kg) cooking apples
1lb (450g) pears
2lb (900g) tomatoes
1lb (450g) chopped dates
2lb (900g) granulated or brown sugar
1tsp cayenne pepper
2tsp mixed spice
1tsp cinnamon
1tsp ginger
1tsp salt
20fl oz (600ml/1pt) malt vinegar

Peel, core and chop the apples and pears.

Skin, deseed and chop the tomatoes.

Put the apples, pears, tomatoes and remaining ingredients into a large pan and bring to the boil. Simmer gently until the fruit and vegetables are tender and the chutney is thick, with no liquid lying on the top.

Pour into clean, warm jars, filling right to the top. When cold, cover and label.

COUNTRY · CUTTINGS

Uncle Walter's wisdom:
Cure for a sore throat –
'Dip a goose's feather in lard and rub it on the back of yer throat.'

'Button yer coat. Do up yer collar. Wild geese about. Bad weather to follow.'

Granny Perkins used to say,
'It's not the man who has the most
That gives the most away.
It's not the man who knows the most
That has the most to say.'

Stuff the body cavity of a pheasant with a large cooking apple to moisten the bird while roasting.

Savoury Sausage and Apple Plait

SERVES 4–5

This keeps well in the freezer and is ideal for a quick meal at home or for a picnic. It is particularly good with Spicy September Chutney.

1 small onion, chopped
1tbsp oil
2 sticks celery, washed and diced
1 small apple, peeled and chopped
1lb (450g) sausagemeat
1tsp ground thyme
salt and pepper
1 medium size egg, beaten
½tsp mild curry powder
8oz (225g) puff pastry, home-made or frozen

Fry the onion in the oil until soft and add the celery, apple, sausagemeat, thyme, seasoning, half the egg and the curry powder. Allow to cool a little. Roll the pastry out into a rectangle, then spread the mixture down the centre of the pastry.

Brush the remaining edges of the pastry with beaten egg and make a series of diagonal cuts at ¾in intervals down the longest sides of the rectangle. Starting at one end, fold the strips over, overlapping in the centre to form a plait. Continue until the filling is completely covered.

Paint the plaited top with beaten egg and bake in a preheated oven at 425°F/220°C/Gas 7 for 15 minutes. After this time, reduce the heat and cook for a further 20 minutes until the pastry is crisp and golden.

Serve either cold with the chutney or hot with braised red cabbage and a baked potato.

Strawberry and Apple Crumble with Nutty Topping

SERVES 8

An all-time favourite at Home Farm, this can be made with frozen fruit just as successfully as fresh. And it takes hardly any time to make the crumble in a food processor.

4oz (100g) butter
6oz (175g) plain flour
2oz (50g) ground almonds
1oz (25g) chopped hazelnuts
1oz (25g) medium oatmeal
6oz (175g) demerara sugar
2lb (900g) Bramley apples, peeled and cored
a little water
8oz (225g) late strawberries, with 2–3oz (50–75g) sugar or to taste

To make the crumble mixture, rub the butter into the flour until it resembles fine breadcrumbs. Add the ground almonds, chopped hazelnuts, oatmeal and sugar and mix together well.

Thickly slice the apples into chunks and put into a large saucepan with a scant half cupful of water. Heat gently until the apples have begun to soften, then stir in the sugar and strawberries and remove from the heat.

Spoon the fruit into a large ovenproof dish. When cool, sprinkle the crumble mixture on to the fruit and lightly press it down. Place in a preheated oven at 350°F/180°C/Gas 4 and bake until golden-brown, about 40 minutes. Serve with dollops of Pat's creamy yogurt.

INDEX